Bloomer's
Developmental
Neuropsychological
Assessments

Volume II

Assessing Basic Executive Learning Processes:

Individual Short Term Memory

Richard H. Bloomer Ed.D. M.S. FACAPP,
Certified Neuropsychologist
Emeritus Professor
The University of Connecticut

ISBN 978-0-9997244-5-3
Short Term Memory, Executive Processes, Neuropsychological assessment, Curriculum

That which we habitually call Short Term Memory is not memory at all. It is a temporary neural excitation, which fades rapidly. It acts as a venturi, a gateway to control the flow of information and limit confusion. Short Term Memory could be more profitably be seen as a defensive measure to prevent stimuli from overwhelming the capacity of the brain to process information.

Bloomer's Developmental Neuropsychological Assessments (DNA)

Introduction to the DNA Series of Volumes

Developmental Neuropsychological Assessment

> *Until recently, ascribing a particular aspect of behavior to an unobservable mental process - such as selective attention- removed the problem from direct experimental analysis. The ability to locate mental functions to particular regions of the brain whose activities can be monitored allows even complex cognitive processes to be studied directly. (Eric Kandel, 1992.)*

Kandel's comment ushered in a new era for psychological assessment. The century old standby's comparing patients to the "norm" are fading. Instead of attempting to squeeze patients into in unruly categories, we have begun to explore the individual mental processes within the patient's nervous system. This evolving process assessment era provides the advantage of allowing the psychologist a reliable view of the specific mechanisms underlying behavior, and the further advantage that most of these mechanisms respond to specific treatments. I have chosen in the Bloomer's DNA assessments to deal with those variables which primarily contribute to verbal learning and memory.

Why are we doing this?
Bloomer's Developmental Neuro-psychological Assessments (DNA)is a series of mental or cognitive measures designed to probe the processes essential to verbal learning. The DNA is a sequence of tools to determine an individuals facility with a number of significant neurocognitive executive processes essential to verbal learning and by inference most school type learning. The DNA battery of tests is a departure from the tests we are accustomed to which focus on declarative knowledge, such as vocabulary, or facts, or, tests that infer s skill level with broad complex processes like reading comprehension. The DNA tasks parse out known contaminants and systematically select, activate, and evaluate the efficiency of specific neural channels, to reveal the efficiency of simple neuro-cognitive process or operation. This approach is it allows the clinician flexibility and a much more specific diagnosis and allows focused treatment to remediate specific operations or knowledge.

Processing tests are not neural localization tests which point to effected parts of the neural anatomy. The DNA instead seeks to explore the efficiency with which the brain performs certain standard tasks. As such information from the DNA is of great value to anyone attempting to restore or build mental function, and to teachers, especially special education teachers, and rehabilitation therapists charged with improving the performance of children in academic type verbal tasks.

The DNA includes nine volumes. Each of the Nine volumes contains complete separate stand-alone instruments which may be chosen by the psychologist to probe specific executive processes. The Assessments are interrelated to give a complete picture of the client's neuro-cognitive executive functions for verbal learning. Each volume also provdes several independent probes of various aspects of the same general theme to provide a more complete picture of the breadth of the client's skills. The scores for these DNA assessments are sufficiently reliable to use for clinical decisions by themselves without resorting to compound or global scores and thus losing specificity of the assessment

A note in passing: I have been following this research thread for some 60 years now I have found the pursuit of neuropsychological assessment variables fascinating. I realize I have only begun to probe the great potential of processing assessment of human brain.

Introduction
All learning rests on three basic executive processing skills:

> **1. Imitation:** (the ability to do what you are told to do Auditory/verbal, Auditory motor) ,

> **2. Copying:** the ability to follow a pattern, visual/motor, visual/verbal (reading) and

> **3. Multiple Discrimination:**, the ability to reliably tell one stimulus from another and to act differentially to different stimuli. Beyond these basics which normally begin to develop at birth or shortly thereafter and progress rapidly at first and gradually more slowly as the brain sheds or inhibits the myriad of possible alternate

connections down, to an efficient few that allows us to stabilize behavior within our culture.

By the time a learner reaches school age we have usually determined that these three processes are in tact. The purpose of schooling is to develop, refine, and enhance a number of additional mental processes which allow the learner to approach and solve more and more complex problems. These processes are sequentially interdependent. That is, is takes a certain level of skill at a lower order component skill in order to recognize and attempt to learn the higher order process. The DNA focuses sequentually on processes essential to verbal learning in a developmental sequence which reflects the interaction between processing skill and neural development.

Bloomer's DNA is divided into nine volumes. I have based the assessments in this series on common tools, some slightly modified to increase reliability and to parse out the mores subtle basic processes. This set of explorations is developmental, interdependent, and cumulative in the sense that one must achieve a certain level of mastery of one task before the next task can be successfully performed. For example, since stimuli in Short Term Memory fade relatively rapidly one must achieve a certain level of response speed with the stimuli in order to maintain stimuli long enough to be acted upon, by the same token one must achieve a STM capacity of at least 3 units for learning simple letter/sound correspondences in reading; one for the visual letter, one for the auditory sound, and one for the process of putting them together.

The several volumes of the DNA are described as follows:

Volume 1. Individual Response Speed: The response speed to a stimulus class is largely dependent upon two factors. The first, the actual experience with the stimulus and the second the structure or the facility of the individual nervous systemThe tasks in this volume index that basic speed of neural transmission. We then remocv the individual differences in response speed which allows us to explore further the variables of Persistence, Automaticitry, Arousal Need, and Purposeful Association

Volume 2. Individual Short Term Memory (STM): STM is a capacity measure of the amount or number of stimuli which may be apprehended or acted upon at one time. It acts as a gatekeeper to prevent the brain from being overwhelmed by stimulation. The four tasks in Volume 2 allow the comparison of auditory and visual stimulation, and written and verbal responding both with and without sequencing. Resting in part on the response speed of the nervous system, and upon the familiarity with the stimuli is a limiting system to control the rate of stimulation that reaches the brain. STM is dependent in part upon the response speed. Since stimuli fade at a rapid rate, a certain minimal level of response speed is required to insert or maintain items in short term memory. Volume 2 also provides us indices of a learner's Impulsivity, Rehearsal Efficiency, and Sequencing in Short Term Memory

Volume 3. Basic Reading Skills: The third requisite for progress within our education system is a set of skills and knowledge that comprise at least the bare minimum for independent reading. These include knowledge of the letters and phonemes in the language (a multiple discrimination task), the ability to blend these into knowledgeable words, the sufficient capacity to spell short words, and the ability to read those few frequent words that do not follow simple phonetic patterns.

Volumes 4,5,6. Memory: represent the intersection between type of learning and memory. Once the basic input skills have developed the next concern is with long term storage or memory. There are two types of memory which were first delineated in the third century B.C. by Aristotle . Each type of learning has developed into a philosophical approach to learning and has it's strong adherants or followers

1. Natural, or happenstance memory rests primarily on Association by stimulus similarity, or on the chance Contiguity of stimuli in time and space memory (Volume 5) and,

2. Purposeful memory or memory as an artifice. I have chosen two common patterns forms of artificial memory to explore; Serial Learning (Volume 4) and Paired Associate Learning (Volume 6):

Volume 4. Natural memory (Association) develops without any necessary forethought or intention on the part of the learner to learn. It is basically wired in and so occurs without thought or direction. It's formation is largely pre-vocal, the result of vetting stimuli by the limbic system. It is primarily a product of interaction with stimuli in the world. The basic main mechanism is contiguity, the happenstance occurrence of stimuli in the same time and space serves to connect them. In addition to contiguity stimuli tend to be associated by similarity on one or more dimensions. Natural memory is fluid, and more fun. Natural memory is also responsive to the next stimulus or to the physical condition of either the surround or the learner, and often unreliable. Many adherents to this form of learning feel strongly that it is natural, unfettered, and leads to creativity. On the other hand contiguity is uncontrolled, is often random, and more often leads to myth and superstition.

Volume 5. Artificial Memory (1) Serial learning, is the purposeful learning sequences or ordering of stimuli or responses. These sequences aid in recall and allow one to perform tasks with less effort and more accuracy. While serial learning facilitates response chains necessary for efficient responding to more complex materials, the serial skill is the basis of most human complex operations and is a fundamental problem solving skill.

Volume 6. Artificial Memory -(2): Paired Associate learning. Paired Associate learning is forming a deliberate connection between two stimuli. Paired associate learning is the most effective procedure for learning factual materials foreign language Vocabulary, Science facts Flerign Language Vocabulary, or any factual material deemed worthy of long term retention

Purposeful memory is often criticized because it requires considerably more effort than Natural memory, however artificial memory is a skill and is responsive to learning and repetition and becomes much easier as it is practiced. Artificial memory processes are important for stable information important enough to retain for any period of time. In addition practicing these procedures also reinforce the executive functions which make putting things in memory much more facile..

Volume 7 Complex Hiearchical Processes: Given the severe limitations in the amount of information that may be active in the human brain at ant given time, a method of compounding information into simpler bundles is essential for manipulating large quantities of information. The most commonly used method is the development of conceptual hierarchies based on a common feature   Volume 5 is a series of assessments that are exploring Higher order processes that manipulate or change the data from the input to output. Concept Formation, Concept Production, Concept Synthesis,

Volume 8 Connotative Meaning; we explore the operations of the amygdala, hippocampus and the limbic stimulus vetting system in this volume. We attempt to penetrate into the learner's awareness of the pre-vocal aspects of stimulus processing. We assess tools for awareness of word Familiarity, Active/Passive, Strong Weak; Sonic Affect, Emotional Ratio, and Imagery. While these assessments are rarely performed they contribute more than 20 % of the variance in such criterion measures as reading comprehension and probably deserve more attention than they currently draw.

Volume 9 Sharpening Up old Tools. A number of assessment tools in curent use hark back a century or more. Many of these have marginal relibilities or have the potential to provide us will additional inforlation   I have assumed the bravado of altering some of these instruments with a view of making them more useful or more stable. This volume includes several tasks dependent upon the perceptual and tracking abilities of the learner. Regard Five Point Test, modified Burtt Letter Maze, Modified Stroop Test, Reverse Spelling.

I have revised several common perceptual tasks to increase reliability and to parse out several variables not found in the original tasks. Included in this volume are a Modified Gauthier's Bells test by enlarging the test to cover more of the visual field and changed it to increase reliability and to indicate the perceptual search sequence in more normal clients as well as retaining it's original intent to assess hemianopia. In stroke and brain damaged individuals

I have also included a Modified Line Bisection, was modified to contrast perceptual accuracy between each hand and increase reliability. Scoring has been modified to jnd's rather than millimeters to compensate for line size and increase accuracy of scoring

There is a Modified The Trails, Tests A, and B were expanded to increase reliability. We are also able to parse out basic response speed to get a reliable estimate of the effectiveness basic search process

Acknowledgments

This work is hardly mine alone. The science of learning and memory reaches back well beyond the recorded history of man. It rests on the work of many scholars and scientists reaching back into antiquity.

Donders, Galton, Ebbinghaus, Weber and Fechner, and Osterman, true exploreres of humam learning science are my immediate precursors. My own explorations of human learning have been marked by wonderful experiences. I was fortunate to have S.D.S. Sprague as a teacher in my first psychology class. He imprinted the scientific method on my young mind.

At Teachers College, Edward L. Thorndike and Irving Lorge shaped my scientific attitude. Robert S. Woodworth never let me forget that there is an "Organism" between the "Stimulus" and the "Response." Percival Symonds provided encouraging mentorship and laboratory space for my early experiments in human learning.

Much credit is due to Irving Lorge who selected me from hundreds of graduate students for his special gruff attention, and weekly thrust upon me, impossible tasks, one after another. One did not fail Dr. Lorge Irving. Lorge was my dragon, whose early demise has left a bewildering emptiness

It was Nick Goldberg who opened the fascinating world of the nervous system and this work owes a great debt to his tutelage

To my supportive partner, Jan Maya Schold, who gives me the space to think and create and an occasional jog to spur me on. Jan Maya. chipped in many of her precious hours to find and correct my many mistakes .

Within my personal experience. my grandfather Hermon Hutcheson pounded into my wandering pre-adolescent mind his mantra, "There ain't no such word as can't."

Last, and perhaps most important, was my own wicked step mother, Marguerite Barnes Bloomer, who with boundless patience first taught me "how" to learn. She also taught me, that "Learning is not fun." Learning is hard work; it is the accomplishment that is exhilarating, rewarding beyond all else..

Bloomer's
Developmental
Neuropsychological
Assessments,
(DNA)

Preface

These several volumes of unique DNA assessment tools set out to explore the neuro-cognitive processes that underlie human learning in the school setting. For that reason they are limited primarily to language learning activities. The DNA assessments expose a deeper layer of cognitive processing than the usual intelligence, psychological, or academic type tests. They generate more specific diagnostic information which allows the development of successful treatments specific to the cause of the learner's problem.

These DNA assessment tools have wide application in any instance where verbal learning is at question. Were we to explore other areas such as mathematics, or music, or athletics the form of these explorations might be very different.

A little history

My own thinking about neuro-cognitive processes harks back to 1948 in a graduate class at Columbia University in experimental psychology taught by Robert S. Woodworth. Dr. Woodworth continually admonished us that, there was an "Organism" in between the Stimulus and the Response. To his way of thinking, important transitions and processes happen within the brain and nervous system induced by stimulation and affecting the very nature of the resulting response.

In that era psychologists were largely divided between the symbolic pseudo-scientific psychology of Freud, and the data driven Stimulus→Response theorists like Pavlov, Thorndike, Skinner, and Guthrie. Most of the S→R theorists tended to disregard these internal organismic changes. Professor Skinner dealt with the internal organism concern by simple stating that the inner world was just like the outside world, and thus psychologists need not be concerned with the organism. Although I became proficient in Mr. Skinner's Behaviorism there was always that niggling of Professor Woodworth's S→O→R theory in the background.

Let us think about Professor Woodworth "O," the Organism between the Stimulus and the Response. While what goes on inside the organism was totally confounding in 1950. Neuroscience now affords us the beginnings of an understanding. We knew then, that if you repeat a response it becomes faster and more efficient. We have actually known that since ancient times, but now we know that this efficiency is caused by the neurons actually growing closer together and their nerve endings producing greater amounts of neuro-transmitters, so that learning and repetition forms a pathway or a network through the maze of neurons in the brain and body. In essence the learning establishes neuro-cognitive processes, or data processing subroutines in the brain, that direct, speed, or inhibit the learning. These neuro-cognitive processes are mostly independent of content, but put together in an appropriate order by the prefrontal cortex, allow for complex problem solving.

It is measuring the efficiency these data processing habits, or neuro-cognitive processes, which are reflected in the efficiency of a learner's scholarship, that are the subject of these several volumes of Developmental Neuropsychological Assessments, (DNA)

Learning applied to Education
A second impetus for these neuro-cognitive process assessments came when I decided to devote my energies to helping children, by leaving the laboratory, and working in the field of education.

In the early 1960's I was tasked to teach a graduate course in Learning for educators. Having been trained in the science of learning I assumed that Verbal Learning was the basic science of Education. I anticipated that future teachers and school administrators would be somewhat knowledgeable and welcome learning more of the scientific underpinnings of their craft.

The reality was quite different. By this time in the 1960's the science of learning had reached a point where, given a specific learning task, one could largely determine that there are several greater or lesser effective methods for teaching that task, and one could fit the method to the student and the circumstance.

My education students seemed completely unaware that there was a science of learning. For them, learning happened when you exposed children to stimulation. The more stimulation, the better the class. I discovered that educators were a faddish lot. At any given period there is only "One Way" to teach. In the early 1960s, that one way was "Class Discussion." Lecture was out. Reward was considered bribery. Rote learning or memorization was anathema. Asking questions might embarrass or stress a student. Demonstration and Audio-Visual was OK, but only as a stimulus for Class Discussion. Playing in class was OK because it was individual expression, and the child was not being coerced into following someone else's ideas.

Personally, I felt a good teacher should be a methodological virtuoso, proficient in a number of methods, and able to adapt method to the learner's circumstance. To foster this idea, and to expose my students to some ideas beyond their current educational fad, I developed a laboratory manual for that learning course, consisting of several modified classical psychological learning experiments. Each learning student was required to give this set of ten tasks to four persons of any age for four trials, to demonstrate the different ways of presenting materials for learning. Student responses to a laboratory manual in a graduate education course were widely varied. Several students

complained bitterly to the Dean about burdensome homework. A good number just performed the task as just another step on the way to their degree. My reward came when an occasional student said "I never knew children could learn like that."

The benefit of all those laboratory manuals to an nerdy scientific type like me was, they contained data! Admittedly student assignments were more than somewhat specious, but I could not help myself from processing it into Means and Standard Deviations by grade, and found interesting developmental trends. These early student assignments allowed me to refine these tasks into an highly reliable learning processes assessment tool, which I called the Bloomer Learning Test od (BLT).

Fortunately this was during the early times of Special Education law and Schools were required to test children for special education. I mustered us as many student helpers as I could, called in as many favors as possible and tested whole schools with the BLT. Over the course of a couple of years we were able to test more than three thousand children and adults with all or part of the learning tasks. I found the test results made explaining, why a child was having learning problems in school very easy, and prescribing appropriate steps to help him could be clearly defined.

The results were exciting. Each task showed developmental improvement over time until adulthood. Further each task showed a growth spurt at some time during pre-adolescence and they seemed to occur in sequence according to task type or complexity that related to children's typical developmental activities. The tasks each related significantly to achievement test data and together predicted academic achievement much better than the traditional IQ test. Further I explored the reliability of the tasks and found most of them high enough to use as an assessment tool for individual students. After perhaps forty years experience with the

BLT, and a certificate program in Neuropsychology with Nick Goldberg I was able to see some of the neurological implications of the BLT and thus spent several years adapting it into a Developmental Neuropsychologicay Assessment (DNA).

Over the next nearly fifty years the DNA has been used by psychologists in schools and clinics all over the U.S. and Canada. It has been revised and refined several times. The DNA offers the clinician a unique view into the mental processing of an individual learner's. The resulting Developmental Neuropsychological Assessment, allows the neuro-psychologist sensitive empirical evidence of the learner's skill with dozens of neuro-cognitive processes and presents a unparalleled tool for treatment design and follow up. The DNA offers the clinician a unique view into the processing of an individual clients learning related mental processes.

RHB 2017

CONTENTS

Volume 2 Preface

.... -1-

Introduction.. -6-

Background .... -6-

Brief History of Short Term Memory .... -7-

Immediate memory span, span of attention .... -7-

Short Term Memory .... -7-

Multiple Memory Systems .... -8-

How much stimulation .... -11-

Age and STM Capacity .... -15-

Response Speed and STM .... -20-

Apprehension Span .... -20-

Memory Capacity .... -23-

Connecting letters and sounds .... -24-

Learning Skills .... -24-

Volume 2 - STM Assessments .... -25-

Task 1. Visual/ Written STM .... -26-

Task 2. Auditory/written STM .... -26-

Task 3. Visual Simultaneous/ written STM ... -26-

Task 4. Auditory/Verbal STM .... -27-

Task 5. Visual/Verbal STM .... -27-

STM and Stimulus/response medium .... -27-

Neurology of Short Term Memory .... -29-

The Visual Neural Channel .... -29-

The Auditory Neural channel .... -29-

Response Differentiation .... -30-

Application of Short term Memory .... -33-

What about Children's Short Term Memory
capacity .... -33-

STM and Learning requires energy .... -34-

Leaning how to learn .... -35-

What does all this mean to the child learning to
read? .... -35-

Increasing Familiarity .... -37-

Influence of STM on learning problems .... -38-

STM and Prediction of Reading and Spelling test
performance .... -41-

Spelling word length, Word Frequency and STM-41-

Digit Span type as a prediction Measure .... -42-

Increasing Familiarity .... -43-

STM Tasks: .... -43-

STM Stimulus Rules .... -44-

STM Learner Rules .... -45-

Task Administration .... -47-

Processing in Short-Term Memory .... -47-

Visual Short Term Memory (VSTM .... -47-

Auditory Short Term Memory (ASTM .... -47-

Visual Apprehension Span (VAPP .... -48-

Auditory-Verbal Short Term Memory (AVSTM)-48-

Visual-Verbal Short Term Memory (VVSTM) . -48-

Processing in Verbal Short Term Memory .... -48-

Interpretation of Volume 2

STM Derived Executive Processing Scores.... -51-

2.7 Stimulus Complexity Ratio: .... -56-

Interpreting Stimulus Complexity .... -56-

2.8-2.11 Working Memory .... -57-

Working Memory: .... -57-

MEASURING Working Memory .... -59-

Interpreting Working Memory .... -60-

2.12 Impulsivity .... -63-

TBI and Head Injury and Impulsivity .... -66-

Testosterone and impulsivity .... -66-

Alcohol and increased impulsivity ...... -67-

Interpreting Impulsivity Scores .... -67-

2.13 Rehearsal .... -68-

Rehearsal vs. Repetition .... -68-

Measuring Rehearsal Effects .... -70-

Interpreting Rehearsal Scores .... -71-

Rehearsal in the classroom .... -72-

Repetition and Satiation .... -74-

Neuro-imaging evidence .... -75-

2.14-2.16 Stimulus-response modality .... -77-

2.15 Cross-modal Comparison .... -77-

Interpretation .... -78-

2.16 Stimulus Mode .... -78-

2.17 Response Mode .... -80-

Interpreting Response Mode .... -81-

2.18- 2.20. Short Term Memory Sequencing . -82-

Scoring Sequencing .... -82-

Interpretation of Sequencing Scores ... -84-

Sequencing as an independent Process -85-

Sequencing vs. Seriation .... -86-

Sequencing is positional not temporal . -87-

Sequencing and seriation are different
processes .... -87-

Sequencing and Handicaps .... -89-

Anxiety, Depression and Short Term Memory -90-

Verbalization, Memory, and Anxiety .... -92-

ADHD and Language problems .... -93-

Memory and the Elderly .... -93-

2.19 Working Memory Sequencing Ratio .... -94-

Appendix A

KR-21 Reliability .... -116-

Standard Error of Measurement .... -116-

Minimum Significant Difference .... -116-

Appendix B .... -124-

RAW SCORES
    INTO
       STANDARD SCORES .... -124-

Appendix C
Visual-Written
Short Term Memory Sstimili

Examiner's Directions .... -146-

INITIAL DIRECTIONS .... -146-

SPECIFIC Task DIRECTIONS .... -147-

    Task 1   VSTM .... -147-

    Task 2 ASTM .... -267-

    Task3, VAPP .... -277-

    Task 5 VAPP .... -315-

Student Answer Forms .... -341-

Examiner Forms .... -341-

Bloomer's Developmental Neuropsychological Assessments (DNA)

Volume 2 Preface

Bloomer's Developmental Neuropsychological Assessments (DNA) is a series of independent tasks designed to activate one or several specific neurocognitive process which underly learning in both children and adults. Most neurocognitive processes improve with age and practice up to some terminal level. We present developmental scaling as a base from which to interpret, and to compare relative efficiency between neurocognitive processes

Many learning problems result when the brain does not process information in a manner to arrive at a satisfactory solution. The ability of the DNA to probe more deeply into the neuro-cognitive processes underlying human learning allows us to design specific treatments, or compensations, for inefficiency in processing and. focus on the specific individual learning process.

How much stimulation can the learner process at one time?

The brain is constantly besieged by boundless stimulation. To make the brain respond to this massive variety of stimulation would produce little but chaos. The brain itself is largely composed of inhibitory neurons. In addition the brain uses several mechanisms to reduce conflicting signals and allow us to focus. The first of these is sensory limitation. Vision is limited to a few angstroms. Sounds below 16hz or above about 25000hz are not perceptible. Second, most of the neurons in the brain are inhibitory. In a perverse sort of way, action itself normally involves inhibition of these inhibitory neurons. Third, the amount of stimulation that reaches the brain is greatly restricted by a mechanism we have come to call Short Term Memory.

Let's talk about neurons, and how they work for a bit. Every thing we do, or don't do is dependent upon neurons which carry an electro-chemical charge from one place to another usually to another neuron or into some network of neurons.

The function of the neuron is a highly complicated electro-chemical reaction. We will be primarily concerned with the relationship of the firing of a neuron to the time involved. In essence I am presenting a very simplified sketch of the firing of a neuron along an axon. This takes time, bth a stimuation time and a refractory time while the neuron returns to normal

Neurons are bathed in a fluid called cytosol which is essential for their function. During firing, positive potassium ions are pumped sequentially out of the neuron, along the neuron's axon into the cytosol. This increases a negative charge in the neuron which travels at the rate of about 0.0625sec/meter down the neuron down the neuron toward the axon end. When this negative impulse reaches the axon end it stimulates the release of neurotransmitters which flow through the cytosol in the gap or synapse and lock on the dendrites of the next neuron to stimulate it

A neuron is not just an on/off switch like your home electricity. After a neuron has discharged the neuron has some clean up to do. Potassium ions must re-enter the axon to bring the electrical charge back to normal. The floating neurotransmitters must be swept up back into the axon end, or destroyed by especially designed chemicals. In essence the stimulation gradually fades sequentially along the chain of neurons that were stimulated. During this refractory period while the neurons return to their resting charge; similar to the after-image you get from staring at a light bulb. I am positing that this fading neural stimulation is an analog of Short Term Memory.

Of course the actual firing of a neuron is a much more

complicated process than I have described, but for our purposes this simpler explanation will suffice.

Thus the STM is a temporally limited holding situation for a limited sequential number of stimuli while decisions about what to do with them can be made. When the stimulation exceeds, in number or complexity, of this STM capacity, the overload causes the release of the stress hormone, Acetylcholine (ACh) which in turn causes great loss of items from STM, and sometimes collapse of the total specific memory structure accompanied by emotional disruption such that little or nothing of the STM stimulation is retrievable and may have long term effects on learning.

STM and Education
Since STM is the aperture to the brain, it controls the maximum size, number, distractions, or speed of stimulation that may be effectively presented to an individual learner. For teachers, of children in the early grades particularly, awareness of each individual learners STM capacity is essential for adjusting presentations of curriculum materials for successful learning. Unfortunately this adjustment is not simple. STM Capacity varies with both the input and output medium, the stimulus type, and the familiarity with the stimulation, not to mention the learner's emotional state, the maturity and the genetic propensities.

I should comment that, in over fifty years of assessing learning problems of children and youth, the most common underlying cause for reading, attention, arithmetic and language problems lies in a failure to adapt the school's ongoing curriculum to individual learner's STM capacity. Many teaching methods and most commercial curricula in the lower grades consistently present learning materials which overload many children's ability to absorb the material. Those children whose STM capacity is consistently overwhelmed become our reading failures, special education students, and depressives who might otherwise have been spared the stigma and emotional turmoil, if their learning materials were more closely adjusted to their abilities.

On the other hand presentation of too few stimuli to those children with more advanced abilities results in boredom and restlessness, from lack of challenge, These children often feel school is not providing anything of value. Matching the curriculum to the learner's STM in the classroom is a fine balancing act especially with the demands of the static curriculum which marches inexorably toward set goals at years end.

Volume 2 provides reliable measures of verbal STM, most commonly applicable in the school learning setting. Since much of school learning is conducted in language, we have limited our STM measures to single letters and short words to provide information to allow for critical adjustments especially in the early years. Further in schools, most language presentation is either auditory or visual and most responses are either written or verbal. We assess five different STM combinations to allow teachers to adjust presentations between input/output media. In addition to allowing for comparison between input/output mode Volume 2 also allows us reliable measures of Impulsivity, Rehearsal Efficiency, Sequencing in STM, and Most important gives evidence to prevent the effects of stimulus overload.

This Volume 2 was written to give neuro-psychologists school psychologists and teachers, specific knowledge of each child's individual capacity to absorb new language learning material. It allows adjustment the presentation of learning materials to improve the success rate of learners in schools.

RHB
Willimantic CT
2017

Volume 2. Short Term Memory

Introduction to Short Term Memory Assessment

Background

Memory is our connection with our past. Without memory, experience affords no recapitulation, and we are committed to vulgar life, full of surprise without moderation. The ability to maintain a stimulus in ones mind after the stimulus event has passed is the basis of all learning. Memory is critical for intelligence, self concept, social skills and civilization itself.

The capacity of the an individual's short term immediate memory span is the gatekeeper to learning. This ability to maintain a stimulus in immediate memory is dependent upon a wide variety of conditions, some controllable, some not. As you shall see genetics and neurological development are among the variables over which we have little direct control. On the other hand stimulus size, stimulus channel, stimulus number, stimulus complexity, stimulus familiarity, response requirements, cognitive processing patterns, meaningfulness, and rate and frequency of presentation are measurable and more flexible. These last are primarily curriculum variables which can and should be altered to enhance the individual learners chances of acquiring and maintaining a stimulus event.

Progress in school, in fact the concept of schooling itself, is dependent upon the capacity of child to attend, to focus upon, and hold stimulation in his mind. The large proportion of this stimulation given the limitations of modern school curriculum is auditory or visual language. The school child whose STM for language stimuli is smaller than the curriculum demands is at a distinct disadvantage and prone to emotional distress.

Brief History of Short Term Memory Explorations

Immediate memory span, span of attention
Memory has always seemed somewhat more complex than simply bringing up images in the mind from the past. Among the first of these differentiations was between material which has been maintained for some long period of time, or Long Term Memory (LTM) and STM, material which is maintained for some shorter period and then forgotten

Short Term Memory
Stemming from these roots is the concept of Short Term Memory (STM), seen as an individual's limited capacity to hold concurrent stimuli for a limited time. The modern STM as a concept is usually attributed to a seminal paper by Atkinson and Schiffren (1967). Their efforts resulted in numerous attempts to chart the course of information from sensation to perception to STM and thence through learning processes to long term memory. This work was critical to the transition of psychology, from the study of learning to the study of cognition. STM or Immediate memory is individual, depending on item type and the individuals experience and maturation, and dependent upon environmental and presentation conditions. STM follows a complex set of rules:

A similar concept is that of immediate memory. According to

Woodworth (1938) the term was coined by Jacobs in 1897, who reports the use of serially presented random numbers as a measure of immediate memory. This concept was adopted by Binet and Simon (1903) and variants of Digit Span, the immediate memory for numbers, has remained as "The Memory" task on many cognitive assessments to this day.

Multiple Memory Systems : One memory or several?
The most common way of discussing memory is as a unity. We talk about our "memory" as good, or bad; as though it is the same for all things and for all modes and implying that memory is singular. This is an offshoot of the, "global" concept of mind which fosters notions of "Intelligence", "Memory" and "Learning" as slightly different ways of regarding the "mass action" of the brain. This global concept leads many psychologists to accept a single score, such as Digit Span, as evidence of "memory." Such a simplistic notion has appeal, and certainly is much easier to conceptualize than a number of "memories". In spite of this popular usage, the evidence, particularly neurological evidence, does not seem to support this unitary position.

Baddeley (1983, 1992 has developed his model for working memory from the original Atkinson and Schiffren (1967) model of STM. The first important contribution of the Baddeley model is the concept of a Central Executive which controls attention and performs an integrating function. Baddeley generates the concept of an active processing STM with his "Central Executive" concept of processing, holding, or changing the STM information. Note this central executive does not differ substantively from the concept of working memory. Prior to this point memory had been largely viewed as a passive repository where things were stored until used or allowed to decay.

Baddeley, (1992) second contribution modifies the generally accepted concept of unitary STM by positing the possibility of more than one channel for memory stimulation. The first of these is a Visual-Spatial Scratch Pad which controls and processes abstract visual and pictorial imagery, and remembrance of location and spatial placement. The second, the Phonological or Articulatory Loop where rehearsal of speech based information keeps the STM memory traces active and is necessary for the acquisition of language. Baddeley's (1983) concepts of "articulatory Loop" and "visual-spatial scratch pad" implied that Visual and Verbal short term memory required different neural networks.

Posner, Stevens, and Raichle (1988) confirmed this position with positron emission tomography (PET Scan) which indicated clearly an increased blood flow to the primary auditory cortex and to Wernicke's area and slight activity in Broca's area when the subject was listening. When the subject was reading there was increased activity in the primary visual cortex in the posterior occipital lobe and activity in the temporal lobe below or inferior to Wernicke's area. Baddeley's contribution was truly that there are multiple memory systems, Spatial &Verbal. There is also separate memory system for each item type, thus there is a different pictorial, spatial, and numerical memory, a kinesthetic memory, and a musical memory to name a few, and they are each different both within and between people.

This concept is not new, but has been lost in the tendency of 20th century psychology to follow the 'g' model and speak of a unitary or single "Memory". William James (1890) in his The Principles of Psychology:. attributes the multiple memories concept to M. Ribot (1885):

We have thus, as M. Ribot says, not memory, so much as memories. The visual, the tactile, the muscular, the auditory may all vary independently of each other in the same individual; and different individuals may have them developed in different degrees. As a rule, a man's memory is good in departments where his interest is strong; but those departments are apt to be those where his discriminative sensibility is high. (James, 1890, p. 685)

Luria (1980) separately studied the four language processes listening, speaking, reading and writing from a neurological viewpoint in regard to topical diagnosis of brain tumors, and verifies processing differences among the four language functions. He states, "As special forms of speech activity, reading and writing differ essentially from spoken speech both in their functional genesis and psycho-physiological structure and in their functional properties" (Luria, 1980, p.528).

Support of this notion has repeatedly demonstrated that the language processing involved with listening, speaking, reading, and writing is different and distinct (Coltheart, 1989). The work of Blumstein (1990), Campbell and Butterworth (1985), and Murdock (1990) documents that the language functions of aphasic patients can be selectively impaired.

Generally Both Miller (1952) and Baddeley were reinventing the wheel from Ebinghaus (1885). Baddeley's contribution was to reawaken psychologists to the fact that there are truly that there are multiple memory systems. Spatial &Verbal. There is also a different memory for pictures, numerical memory and musical memory systems to name a few, and they are all different both within and between people.

Thus, the position we have taken is somewhat different from the traditional view of Short Term Memory. We will not concern ourselves with "Memory" but with differentiating the efficiency between memory systems and fitting the assessment closely to the task. Our concern in this Volume will be limited to the visual and auditory STM systems since these are most commonly used for school type learning.

How much stimulation

I like to look at STM as a capacity measure. How much information can an individual brain input and retrieve in a limited period of time. Although it was neither unique nor new to psychology, a 1952 article by George Miller entitled "The Magic Number 7 plus or Minus 2" received wide press, and thus customarily people tend to think of STM as a fixed number seven.

This simplistic fixation of the "Magic Number" has done a remarkable disservice especially to the development of learning materials for children. STM is developmental. The seven plus or minus two holds only for adult and only if the stimuli are single numbers. The maximum STM is similar for single letters, but if you use words or phrases, it becomes significantly smaller. Miller's argument would have been more reasonably couched as the "Maximum Adult STM".

STM Capacity

Our data on STM for single unrelated letters serially presented indicates this limit is actually 6.9 plus or minus 1.87 for adults. For unrelated four letter words it is 5.5 words plus or minus 1.68 these data are from 1349 cases eleventh grade through age 40. In essence the larger or more complex the stimulation the fewer the number of stimulus units can be processed in STM.

STM and Development

Short term memory for a given class of stimuli changes through learning and development over time. From the beginnings of learning the stimulus class where automaticity or fluency has not been developed, the STM is marked limited. Through synaptic development, an efficient neural circuit results in a gradually increasing memory span while the learning achieves automaticity. During this learning-development period the learner should also develop efficient cognitive processes for handling and manipulating the stimulation. These learning processes are enhanced if the training with the stimuli occurs during the appropriate developmental window which insures that prior contingent processes are developed. In nature this matching with the neurological developmental plan is automatic since awareness of the stimuli is dependent, in part, upon developmental readiness for neuronal connection and prior process efficiency. One problem for some learners, is that the schools requirement for response to excessively numerous and complex stimuli marches on, inexorably, whether the child is developmentally ready or not.

Table below shows the average STM for letters and single four letter words by the grade level. We have used grade level
in lieu if age because the curriculum demands on the learner are customarily made at the grade level

Functional Short-Term Memory (STM) for single letters and common four letter words, mean and standard deviation by grade level for visual sequential, presentation combined (N=1,349)

Grade Level	Number of Students Tested	Average STM for Letters	Standard Deviation Letters	Average STM for Words	Standard Deviation Words
1	138	3.0	1.05	0.96	0.60
2	183	4.1	1.33	1.3	0.88
3	121	5.1	1.13	3.5	0.95
4	189	5.6	.90	3.8	0.82
5	205	5.9	1.43	5.4	1.05
6	249	6.5	1.13	5.0	1.10
7 & 8	82	6.5	1.47	5.0	1.38
9 & 10	81	6.9	1.08	5.5	1.30
11 - age 40	146	6.9	1.87	5.5	1.68

Age and STM Capacity

The amount of material that can be held in STM is much less in children. These data tell us that at first grade level, the STM for unrelated Letters is 3.0 plus or minus 1.05 letters This calculates to mean that 84% of first graders would have an STM capacity of two letters and 96% will have an STM capacity of a single letter

The STM for unrelated four letter words STM is 0.96 words plus or minus 0.6 words. If a single four letter-word is presented, approximately 47% of the children will apprehend it. Even fewer children will apprehend a five-letter word. This means reading programs using full words as a medium for teaching, more than half the first graders do not have sufficient STM capacity to hold a single word long enough to process it. It is significantly worse when phrases, sentences, or "Whole Language" are used as the medium of instruction. Thus stimulus overload is probably the greatest contributor to the poor reading skills that plagues schools across the nation.

STM Overload

STM-overload is perhaps the major contributor to poor school performance. STM is seen as a temporally limited holding situation for a limited number of stimuli while decisions about what to do, or how to process, could be made. STM is readily overloaded by the number or complexity of the stimuli or processes. When this occurs, it causes the brain to raise defensive barriers and thus as the stimulation exceeds the STM capacity the amount retained disproportionately diminishes.

When the stimulation exceeds, in number or complexity, this STM capacity, the overload often causes loss of items from STM, and sometimes collapse of the total specific memory structure so than little or nothing of the STM stimulation is retrievable. Unfortunately STM overload is not without its additional costs in anxiety and reduced self esteem. When confronted with supra-span stimulation the learner learns to approach learning tasks with trepidation and anxiety which further reduces the STM capacity for future stimulation. You will note that looking at this phenomenon from the instructors point of view the learner appears to be inattentive, while from the learner's viewpoint overload causes an increase in anxiety added to the confusion caused by the excess stimulation.

"When the length of the list exceeds the memory span a noticeable increase in difficulty occurs Ebbinghaus (1885) for example was able to recite seven nonsense syllables after one reading, but seventeen readings were required for a list of twelve and 30 readings were required for a list of sixteen." Lyons (1914).

Below is a table taken from an early study by Oberly (1928). It demonstrates the effects of increasing numbers of stimuli in an immediate memory task it shows the number of items presented, the percent correct, and he mean number of unrelated digits recalled. This study demonstrates the results of overloading, or the fading of the initial stimuli during the time required for the presentation, These traces of fading stimulation interfere with apprehension of the stimulus presentation. The one hundred adult learners are members of a lost breed, Experienced Learners. Individuals who practiced continually to develop more effective learning and memory skills

Visual apprehension span for Digits
List length vs lists recalled correct in sequence N=100 <u>adult experienced learners</u>*

Items Presented	1	2	3	4	5	6	7	8	9	10	11	12	13	14
Mean % Correct	100%	100%	100%	100%	95%	88%	70%	52%	30%	22%	0.8%	0.3%	0.2%	0.1%
Mean # Items Recalled	1	2	3	4	4.8	5.3	4.9	4.2	2.7	2.2	0.9	0.4	0.3	0.1

(after Oberly, 1928) (N = 100) memory span for digits by individuals for lists of varying lengths from 1 to 14 digits 5 sessions and 50 lists each, responses in serial order and perfect.

*It should be noted that Oberly used experienced adult learners who had highly developed learning processes. These results are likely much superior than those expected from naive learners or young children.

Overloading the STM actually reduces the amount of information which may be processed, and severe overload, particularly when there is some cost to non-response, generates anxiety which when repeated in good Pavlovian manner becomes attached to memory tasks and may cause the mind seek alternative stimulation or to shut down completely.

Overloading the STM actually reduces the amount of information which may be processed, and severe overload, particularly when there is some cost to non-response, generates anxiety which when repeated in good Pavlovian manner, becomes attached to memory tasks and may cause the mind seek alternative stimulation or to shut down completely. Overload induces activation of stress hormones which in themselves, further inhibit learning and retention. Overload of the learner's STM capacity by curricula and by teachers is the most common cause for school failure. In schools, teachers and curricula both, impose demands on the child's short term memory by proscribing uniformly to the group, the type, and amount of stimulation which must be processed to maintain ones standing in a class. When there is a consistent mismatch between the curriculum learning demands and the child's memory span, the expected learning outcomes are not achieved, and the result often has serious academic, social and emotional consequences for the learner.

STM Half-life
Stimulation is limited temporary excitation of the nervous system. STM is almost always tested by immediate recall within a very few seconds of the stimulus presentation. The stimulus half life is that point where about half the stimulation has faded so that the learner can return only about half of the stimulation presented. The half life of an average STM

stimulus is about usually about eight seconds. This half life is longer or shorter depending upon the stimulus channel, type and familiarity of the material, the complexity of the processing, and the condition and response speed of the learner.

 STM reaches a peak capacity at about 2.5 seconds from the onset of stimulation. Given a learning stimulus the with no other action, that stimulus will soon begin to fade. The stimulation is then gradually erased and becomes difficult or impossible to retrieve. This erasure feature of STM serves the important function of protecting the mind from over-load of non-pertinent information.
It is the duration of this half life that is a determinant of learning effectiveness. In essence the stimulation and the response are limited in the time they are activated and gradually fade to make room for new stimulation.

We must make a distinction between Short Term Memory and learning. Immediate or short term memory (STM) can be viewed as the gateway to learning. STM capacity operationally is the learner's access to information on a temporary basis for a specified immediate retrieval event. To be learned the stimulation must first pass through this limited STM barrier. In essence this Short Term Memory excitation enables learning and at the same protects the brain from over-load.

Response Speed and STM
The speed of neural processing is critical to short-term (or working) memory. Given that STM is limited by time, and Response Speed is related to the rate of processing

stimulation. The greater the learners' response speed the greater the number of stimuli that can be loaded within the time limit of the STM. Thus the interaction between rate and STM is limited in both its time and its capacity to store and process information. Because of the limited response speed or capacity of short term memory, an individual while solving a problem, may overload short-term memory and lose the solution. Furthermore, the information held by the short-term memory decays rapidly unless it is processed or continuously rehearsed. A rapid response speed is one way of overcoming this difficulty, because it allows more material to be input and processed and but STM overload occurs more readily allows the problem to be solved before the information decays.

The conclusion is that the faster the learner's nervous system, the more information it can hold and process before decay. Proponents of this view note that while speed may not be the only factor to reduce the chances of over-load, it is a major contributor (Vernon 1987, pp. 2-3).

Apprehension Span
There is another limitation to memory which infects the learning process, and that is the limited ability of the human mind to process simultaneous information. According to R. S. Woodworth (1938), this was first explored by Sir Robert Hamilton in 1857. Hamilton would throw varying numbers of beans in a box and then ask subjects, in a single glance, to tell the number. He called this procedure the Span of Apprehension and it demonstrates the limitation of the mind to accurately absorb simultaneously presented information. Apprehension span is an analogue for simultaneous visual presentation

Automaticity and Short Term Memory

Automaticity is an over-learned connection between some stimulus and an invariant response. Samuels, (1987) defines automaticity, as a singular well learned neural route between stimulus and response, effects STM. Since these automatic responses require less energy they are both more rapid and the STM capacity for automatic stimuli is greater than for stimuli which are foreign or only partially learned. Samuels (1987) argues that a major factor in reading difficulty is lack of automaticity in letter/sound connections decoding, which overloads the attentional system, places heavy demands on short-term memory, and interferes with comprehension. Rapala, & Brady, (1990) support Samuels position and suggest simplifying or reducing phonological processing requirements in verbal short-term memory will increase available processing resources. They also found developmental increases in verbal short-term memory were accompanied by more accurate and rapid execution of phonological tasks. In essence the more familiar the learner is with the stimuli, the greater the STM capacity for that material.

In essence, if you are patient enough, and take small enough sequential steps you can teach nearly anything to nearly everybody

STM CAPACITY AND SPELLING

Let's get practical for a bit. When assessing a learner, I am never interested in the grade level at which the learner spells. Rather, I want to know whether the learner has the appropriate capacity, and knows 'how to learn' spelling words. The cause of spelling problems with most learners is stimulus overload and lack good learning techniques. These learners have rarely been taught effective mental processes for learning. They simply do not know how to learn to spell a word.

RALPH.

Ralph, a fourth grader, is a case in point. Ralph's school had referred him to a tutor for extra help in learning his weekly spelling words. Every evening, Ralph's mother also worked with Ralph on his spelling list. Even with all this help, Ralph made no progress and always failed the weekly Friday spelling test. The school reported that Ralph was working at grade level in all other areas. An intelligence test showed his IQ to be 121, well above average. A neurological assessment found no reasons for poor spelling. However, Ralph did have problems in the three common areas listed above.

Memory Capacity : Ralph's Short Term Memory was limited to three letters at a time. On tests, he could spell also three-letter words without error, but began misspelling with four letter words. He was completely frustrated by six-letter words. Yet the weekly twenty-five words in Ralph's spelling curriculum averaged seven to eight letters in length. In short, the length of the spelling words, in the curriculum far exceeded

Ralph's memory capacity.

Connecting letters and sounds (phonetic knowledge): In further tests, (DNA Vol.III) Ralph's errors indicated that he did not automatically connect many letters with their sounds. This limited knowledge of letter/sound relationships made it difficult for Ralph to convert spoken words into written letters, and in turn impacted his STM, which in turn limited his spelling and probably his reading also. Ralph scored in the average range on multiple choice reading tests. Ralph was probably guessing on his multiple-choice reading tests, using his intelligence to hide his poor ability to decipher new words.

Learning Skills : Ralph also had extremely poor learning skills. When I asked him to study a list of five words he had already studied and misspelled from his previous week's spelling lesson, he simply sat and stared at the first word on the list. He did not attempt to read the word or the letters, either to himself or aloud, nor did he copy them or practice writing them. After a few minutes, I retested Ralph. Of the five study words, he spelled only one of them correctly—the first one.

I next asked Ralph to study a different word and explain what he was doing to remember the word.

He said, "Look and see if I can remember it."

This answer indicates no real learning strategy except staring at the word. When I asked Ralph to study another list of ten five-letter words and then to just recite verbally them from memory, he again did not attempt to read them aloud, to write them, or to use his memory. He simply stared hard at the list. When quizzed, he was able to verbally repeat only five words.

Like Ralph, many other poor spellers had limited learning skills. They don't know how to learn. Ralph's problem could have ben readily alleviated with a short course in what to do with a new word. Ralph was treated by using the standard learning procedure designed to correct this deficiency in Professor Bloomer's Spelling program. He learned the process of learning or memorizing spelling words. His letter sound connections and his reading skills improved. And his short term memory increased to five or six letters. The procedure can be transferred to many other learning problems.

Volume 2 - STM Assessments

Volume 2 assessments of Short Term Memory assessments are useful primarily for predicting an individual's performance in various visual and auditory language channels customarily employed in school learning. We are interested in assessing and comparing the short term memory for letters and words in auditory, verbal, spoken, and written channels. Volume 2 tests probe five different input/output channels for letters and words which are common in the teaching/learning environment. These tasks so not portend to predict STM for numbers, or music or any other learning media.

Volume 2 probes the following teaching/learning channels:

Task 1. Visual/ Written STM for letters and words: The stimuli are presented sequentially visually in sequences of increasing length and the learner responds by writing.(VSTM). This type of STM is basically copying common in learning to write and spell.

Task 2. Auditory/written STM for letters and words: the stimuli ate presented verbally, in sequences of increasing length and the learner responds by writing. (ASTM). This type of STM requires conversion from auditory to written and is often used in dictation.

Task 3. Visual Simultaneous/ written STM for letters and words: The stimuli are presented in simultaneously in Increasingly more complex arrays and the learner responds by writing (VAPP) related best to reading ability.

Task 4. Auditory/Verbal STM for letters and words: The stimuli ate presented verbally, in sequences of increasing length and the learner responds by speaking. (AVSTM) this is usually the most common STM procedure in the classroom.

Task 5. Visual/Verbal STM for letters and words: The stimuli are presented sequentially visually in sequences of increasing length and the learner responds by speaking. (VVSTM) is an analog for reading aloud.

In general, visual stimuli are learned more effectively than auditory stimulation, in part because visual stimuli tend to be more stable. By the same token written responses are also more effective in part because they involve gross and fine muscle movement in addition to vocalization.

STM and Stimulus/response medium

STM can be used to predict school success. In school learning we are normally concerned with visual or auditory stimulation. STM in not a fixed number for anyone. It varies for individuals by input/output medium The relationship of STM to learning is a little more complicated. It depends upon stimulus type. Generally if the material is new to the learner, auditory stimulation is less effective than visual stimulation probably because visual stimulation is more stable over time. In turn, more information is learned or retained from a written response than with a verbal response. In general visual-sequential stimuli with a written response will produce the best immediate recall. Using STM to predict reading progress requires different STM tasks that prediction of spelling progress. STM for numbers is poorly related to school language tasks. It seems the rule is, the more similar the STM task is to the Criterion task, the better the prediction.

A teacher or a school psychologist should not rely on a single type of STM Measure and should never rely on STM for numbers as your estimate of STM Capacity for general school learning.

In addition to numerical values for various STM measures our data will allow us to parse out several measures of the neurocognitive processes involved in Short Term Memory. Knowledge of overload effects, impulsivity, rehearsal strategies, sequencing and preferred stimulus or response mode developed from the STM Tasks provides teachers and psychologists additional guidance in developing successful individual learning procedures.

Neurology of Short Term Memory

Neurology of Short Term Memory the Visual Neural Channel
the neural route to the prefrontal cortex varies according to the stimulus medium.   Visual input flows from retina by way of the optic chiasm and the lateral geniculate via the optic radii to the occipital lobe. From the occipital lobe, visual language information moves through the inferior temporal lobe, is vetted in the amygdala for emotional value to the temporal pole increasing in complexity and refinement, and thence to the angular gyrus. (Kandell, Schwartz, & Jessell, 1993). This stimulation tends to contain objects to be identified, and it activates the ventral brain which is concerned with "what" (Object recognition, identification of things) temporal lobe neural channels.

The Auditory Neural channel
Auditory stimulation is processed by an entirely separate route from the cochlear nucleus via superior olivary complex and the inferior colliculus in the midbrain to the medial geniculate of the thalamus and thence to Heschel's gyrus in the superior temporal gyrus. This auditory information is refined through area To and reaches the temporal pole where it may or may not merge with visual stimulation.(Kandell, Schwartz, & Jessell, 1992)

Familiar sounds move to the auditory cortex in the superior

gyrus of the temporal lobe and are then processed or refined into "representations" or brain readable code in the auditory association areas. Eventually refined auditory and visual stimulation meet and merge in superior colliculus and the temporo-parietal area near the angular gyrus so that the sight and sound of the stimulation become congruent into a single perceived complex stimulus.

As with the auditory system, there is also an emergency auditory neural circuit. (LeDoux, 1996) Sudden, loud sharp or unexpected sounds proceed without refinement directly from the medial geniculate to the amygdala, which in turn activates the hypothalamus, the cerebellum and the basal ganglia in preparation for "flight, freeze, or fight" or other defensive reactions

Response Differentiation

It is clear that the neural pathways for the visual stimulation and the auditory stimulation are quite separate so too are the neural pathways for verbal and written responses. Differential output requirements of the learning situation, verbal or written require differing neural circuits. Then hand and arm are activated by different sections of the motor strip, but so too is there activation differential motor subroutines in the basal ganglia and coordination of differing neural patterns in the cerebellum.

Verbal response requires activation of sections of the motor planning, and motor activations areas of the motor strip which lead to facial muscles and changing pitch in vocal chords. On the other hand, written response requires activation of a different area of the motor strip leading to nerves which activate the arm and finger muscles used in writing. Both of these operations involve the orderly sequential activation of different subroutines stored in the striatum of the basal ganglia and the cerebellum.

In the Volume 2 Bloomer's Developmental Neuropsychological Assessment manual, STM 5 tasks are designed to probe the neural channels most commonly used in schools. The five tasks are balanced in form so they may be comparable within an individual learner without reference to standard scores. This the learner's strengths and weaknesses on various processing variables are compared to himself and not to some mythical normative population. Further these memory tasks are baseline tasks and are used for comparison with more complex learning tasks and for the development of process indicator scores

These differing neural circuits represent, in part, The relative efficiency of these separate systems controls the input of verbal stimuli and is important comparative information for the psychologist and therapist alike. Comparison between these Developmental Neuropsychological Assessment tasks afford inferences about a number of cognitive processes implicated in processing verbal materials critical to academic success. Wood, Richman, & Eliason, (1989) note that as a group both LD's and Controls performed significantly better on verbally presented items than on visually presented items. Clinically we have supported this concept for groups of LD's but found this difference does not always hold for individual learners.

Short term memory is effected by an interaction between midbrain activation and automaticity of the specific responses. Hence responses, where the neural circuits are young and ill-formed, where neural pruning of alternative circuits is incomplete, require more energy than automatic stimuli, and fewer of them may be processed at one time. Automaticity for more than one stimulus is necessary to develop of Short-Term Memory. The Bloomer's Developmental Neuropsychologica Assessment manual focuses primarily on assessment of verbal behavior related to school learning and hence is largely concerned with the functions of the occipital and temporal lobes.

Application of Short term Memory :

What about Children's Short Term Memory capacity ?

We have a particular interest in short term memory because it is limited in number and size as well as duration. That limitation, in turn, controls the amount of information that may be processed at one time, and ultimately over long periods limits the amount of information in memory. The effectiveness of ones attempts at learning is in large part dependent upon the number, size and complexity of the stimuli that can be maintained at one time.

Functional short term memory (STM), or working memory is a representation of the child's immediate memory capacity, the amount of information a child's mind is open to for learning or remembering. This STM capacity is determined by several variables. Capacity is developmental. STM gradually increases up to age twelve or fourteen as the brain matures. This development differs from child to child so it is related to intelligence test scores.

Functional memory is also influenced by environmental forces. This suggests that teachers may change the short term memory requirements to meet the individual differences of the pupils in her classroom.

STM and Learning requires energy
STM can be seen as the first step in learning, it filters the quantity and type of stimulation so the brain can focus and

further process the stimulation via the hippocampus into LTM. This processing requires additional energy. At some point, after sufficient repetitions when the response to the stimulation becomes automatic the individual achieves a maximum STM span for that class of stimulation and the learner can put more energy into the long term memory processes. These maximums vary from individual to individual and by stimulus size and type, as well as by processing demands. Further, the individual maximum memory span for specific stimuli may diminish by disuse or by neglect over time. Normal recovery from disuse may be rapid,

STM and learning are effected by association with emotional states. Emotional arousal absorbs energy and focus from STM as energy is channeled to the emotional arousing stimulus. Both STM and Learning are diminished by the degree of arousal of either a positive or negative valence. Recovery related to emotional states, or from lack of effective training during the 'developmental window' is usually an arduous rehabilitation task.

Leaning how to learn

What does all this mean to the child learning to read?
No matter the stimulus some children will miss some of the stimuli, or perhaps crucial parts of complex stimuli. How many children might this be? Here the Standard Deviations in our data give us important information. The Standard deviation tells us about the range of children's abilities.

Short Term Memory for Letters and for Words for first and second grade pupils. (N=321)

Grade Level	Number of Students Tested	Average STM for Letters	Standard Deviation Letters	Average STM for Words	Standard Deviation Words
1	138	3.0	1.05	0.96	0.60
2	183	4.1	1.33	1.3	0.88

Letters:

If we look at our table above, at the end of first grade we would expect on average, about fifty percent of the children with similar experiences to return about three letters from immediate memory. The standard deviation of 1.05 tells is that about fifteen percent of the children will return only 2 letters from memory and about 2 percent will return only one, or fewer, letters. Similarly fifteen percent of first grade children will be able to return 4 letters and about two percent have a short tem memory capacity of five letters.

Words:
If the teacher chooses to use whole words as a teaching stimulus, the effectiveness will be quite different. About half (forty-six percent) of the children will return one single four letter word from a presentation of three. A standard deviation of 0.60 indicates about thirty-five percent of children, near the end of their first school year, are unable to return a single common word. Interestingly, this is near the average percent of children in special or remedial education. It is these children who are the future reading problems, the anxious, the remedial readers of the future. It is clear the smaller the teaching unit the greater the success rate. Asking children to learn material which exceeds their memory capacity induces stress.

Changing the stimuli
The ability of the learner to learn depends upon whether the size or complexity of the learning task fits the learners functional STM. The teacher can reduce the size and or the complexity of the material presented the material to assist the struggling student, or increase the size and complexity to maintain the interest of the better performing student. Given the administrative structure and curriculum demands of most schools altering materials to fit each learner's abilities is a difficult task.

Increasing Familiarity
The more familiar the learner is with the material to be learned the greater his STM capacity, within genetic and developmental limits

Influence of STM on learning problems
One of the common processing deficits of dyslexics and individuals with learning disabilities is limited short term

memory which limits their abilities to input information and causes a progressive decline in their academic performance. Below are mean scaled scores on memory tasks for a group of 143 individuals with a learning disability with at least a 1.5 SD discrepancy between reading scores and Intelligence as measured by the Wechsler tests VIQ = 96.5; PIQ = 99.3

Percent Individuals with a Learning Disability Scoring Below One Standard Deviation on Several STM Assessments

STM Presentation Mode	Mean Scaled Score	Expected Standard Deviation -1.0 S.D.= 16%	Actual Percent LD's Scoring Below -1.0 S.D.	S.D.Ratio of LD's to Normal Expectancy
Auditory-Written Sequential	9.02	2.43	24%	1.50
Visual- Written Sequential	8.49	2.30	28%	1.75
Visual-Written Simultaneous	8.50	2.77	32%	2.0

In a normal population we would expect a slightly stronger response after a visual-sequential presentation than from an auditory presentation. These data from adjudicated learning disabled. For the learning disabled sample the table indicates the standard score for all STM tasks is lower than the normal population. This discrepancy is severe in some individuals. In a normal population we expect about 16% of the pupils to score below one standard deviation on STM tasks. The data indicate that between 8% and 16% more Individuals with Learning Disability achieved a scaled score of less than one standard deviation below the expectation for "normal" classroom learners. This limited STM for verbal materials of the learning disabled students has a serious impact on academic performance.

Short Term Memory and Disabled Populations

We have shown that the STM of learning disabilities is diminished. Short term memory deficits are common in children with Learning Disabilities. Siegel, & Ryan, (1989) tested 641 LD and normal readers. and found poor STM related to reading difficulty. A similar result is reported by Bowey, et al, (1992).who found Poor readers had difficulty with verbal working memory.

Levy, & Hobbes, (1989) findings suggest that children with ADD and ADHD may have impaired STM. Routh, (1987). found children with head injury (CHI) show memory problems and along with general cognitive impairment.

Lehman, (1991) and Waldron, & Saphire, (1993) compared gifted LD's with normal children and found Gifted Ss with LD were weaker in verbal short term memory. Short term memory may effect speech acquisition as well. Speidel, (1993) reports a male twin had much more difficulty learning to speak than his twin sister also had a much lower STM and phonological processing.

STM and Prediction of Reading and Spelling test performance
CTBS test scores from in a sample of 523 public school children from schools in Eastern Connecticut ages 6-12, between Visual Apprehension Span (VAPP) and reading and spelling as measures on the CTBS is respectively .63 and .67, and for Visual Written (VSTM) and reading and spelling is respectively .50 and .68 indicating that STM and Reading Skills develop at similar rates.

Spelling word length, Word Frequency and STM
The length of a word is an indicator of both the size and complexity of a stimulus. As such word length effects the STM capacity for the word. Typically for the last century we have used the frequency of occurrence of a word as an indicator of it's spelling difficulty. However, word length is a superior predictor of spelling difficulty than frequency of occurrence. In a random sample of 538 common words the correlation of spelling difficulty and the length of the word (r. =.57; N = 538, 32% of the variance) as compared to word frequency(a rough index of Familiarity) and spelling difficulty (r. = - .36; N= 538, 13% of the variance) (Bloomer 1959).

The number of letters in the word reflects directly the STM capacity required to learn the word This relationship is apparently maintained into adulthood . Ahissar, et-al., (2000) in a study of adults with a childhood history of reading and spelling difficulties and normal controls found poor auditory discrimination in the poor readers even in adulthood.

Digit Span type as a prediction Measure
We have traditionally used auditory-verbal STM measures

such as Digit Span in these studies, however, based on the findings of Ricitelli (1991), eith first grade pupils the relationship with spelling be even stronger for measures of visual-written STM (r. = .71,= 50% of the variance) as compared with the correlation of spelling to auditory-verbal STM (r. = .26,= 7% of the variance). On the other hand using digit span as a predictor produced a correlation of (r.= -.19) negatively related to spelling. It is quite clear that the type of STM task is importan t for predicting the result. The school neuropsychologist should be armed with a reliable visual-written STM measure as the instrument of choice if one is to make inferences about reading, and spelling potential from STM capacity measures

Short Term Memory is related to the complexity of the stimuli presented and the type or class of the stimuli. Thus letters are not processed in the same circuits as numbers and abstract figures are not processed with the same circuitry as either of the others. Memory they may differ widely depending upon the manner in which it is measured.

Potential Treatments:

Changing the stimuli
The ability of the learner to learn depends upon whether the size or complexity of the learning task fits the learners functional STM. The teacher can reduce the size and/or the complexity of the material presented the material to assist the struggling student, or increase the size and complexity to maintain the interest of the better performing student. Given the administrative structure and curriculum demands of most schools altering materials to fit each learner's abilities is a difficult task.

Increasing Familiarity

The more familiar the learner is with the material to be learned the greater his STM capacity, within genetic and developmental limits thus any material that has been recently practiced will tent to have a greater STM

Bloomer's
Developmental
Neuropsychological
Assessment Manual
STM Tasks:

The Bloomer's DNA manual for Volume 2 provides STM assessment of the several neural circuits including auditory and visual areas of the left temporal lobe and connections with the frontal cortex motor areas, which are involved in STM of verbal materials. There are three visual tasks and two auditory tasks, the neural substrates of Baddeley's Visual Spatial Scratchpad and the Articulatory Loop. In addition, two tasks probe the relative efficiency of the verbal output channel and three use the visual neural response channel. The stimuli are restricted immediate memory for letters and words, which are of greatest concern in the school environment. We parse out reliable diagnostic information about the efficiency of several processes basic to short term, and to Working Memory, including Rehearsal, Impulsivity, Cross Modal efficience and Sequencing. To accomplish this task, STM capacity is measured by both visual and auditory stimulation, and verbal and written response, with simultaneous and successive presentation. We have used the written response task VSTM as base line so other measures are relative to the individual learner's basic visual and auditory memory with written response.

The goal of this section is to allow the school neuro-psychologist move beyond the usual misleading general statements of memory ability and to diagnose more accurately; thus to prescribe educational services or rehabilitative treatments specific to an individual learner we are able to explore and compare the following Short Term Memory tasks.

STM Stimulus Rules :

1. The greater the number of stimuli the shorter the half life. Generally a stimulus of eight or ten simple stimuli like letters or single numbers will significantly decrease the half life.

2. For large stimuli or complex stimuli the half life is shorter. The more complex the stimulus the shorter the half life. Words have a shorter half life than letters, Phrases are still shorter. etc. It is easily possible to generate a stimulus so complex or large that the half life is less than zero.

3. Stimulus materials that are customarily sequential will have a longer half life.

4. The more emotionally neutral the stimuli the greater the half life. Intense, strongly positive or negative words induce emotional responses in the limbic system which interfere with leaning

STM Learner Rules :

1. The more facile the learner, (response speed, intelligence, etc), the longer the half life of STM.

2. Familiarity, The more familiar the learner is with the stimulus or the stimulus type, the greater the STM half life.

3. The more experience the learner has with processing similar learning material into LTM , the greater the half life of the STM.

STM Stimulus Presentation Rules

1. Presentation rate of unconnected stimuli at a rate of less than about 1.5 seconds or more than 4 seconds, will shorten, the half life of STM. Two seconds presentation rate appears optimum.

2. Visual stimulation has a longer half life than Auditory stimulation, which in turn has a longer half life than Audio-Visual presentation.

3. Input Stimulation in the same medium as the output responses will have a longer half life.

4. The greater the amplitude of competing stimulation the shorter the half life

Volume 2 STM Task Administration

Processing in Short-Term Memory (5 subtests)
Volume 2 consists of a complete set probes of the auditory and written visual and auditory verbal circuits. The functional capacity of these separate neural routes is critical for planning instruction. The Bloomer's Developmental Neuropsychologica Assessment of short term memory consists of five short term memory tasks assessing the auditory and visual input channel and the verbal and written output channels and for comparing simultaneous and successive stimulus presentation.

We have restricted our memory assessment to letters and words as the most important channels for verbal learning in school. You should not assume that memory for one set of stimuli is equivalent to another. You are referred to other tests for reliable instruments for assessing memory for numbers, sentences or faces depending upon your assessment goals.

2.-Task I   **Visual Short Term Memory (VSTM)** The capacity to hold in STM visual sequentially presented letters and words with immediate written response.
(Appendix C, page 144.)

2.-Task II   **Auditory Short Term Memory (ASTM):** The capacity to hold in STM auditorially presented letters and words with immediate written response.
(Appendix D, page 259.)

2.- Task III   **Visual Apprehension Span (VAPP):** The capacity to hold in STM visual simultaneously presented letters and words with immediate written response. **(Appendix E, page 269.)**

2.-Task IV   **Auditory-Verbal Short Term Memory (AVSTM) :** The capacity to hold in STM auditorially presented letters and words with immediate verbal response. **(Appendix F, page 291)**

2.- Task V   **Visual-Verbal Short Term Memory (VVSTM)** : The capacity to hold in STM visual sequentially presented letters and words with immediate verbal response. **(Appendix G, page 306.)**

2. Student Answer Sheets and Examiner forms. (Appendix H page 331.)

Processing in Verbal Short Term Memory , 12-18 minutes
Multiple memory circuits and the temporal lobes (Bloomer, 1963; 1978,1996; Baddeley, 1983)

Memory Capacity is one of the most important measures of a child's potential. It dictates how much information a child can handle at one time and thus his or her rate of progress in school. We are habituated from the past to think of Short Term Memory as a unitary concept and thus a measure like digit span was seen as an adequate measure of memory, but this is not so.

We now know that different types of information travel different routes in the brain and differing response modes activate differing potions of the motor nerves.   Auditory verbal tasks have been found to be relatively unrelated to reading, but visual simultaneous tasks are highly related. Therefore, we ask children to respond to auditory and visual simultaneous and sequential presentations and to provide verbal and written responses for both letters and words answers questions concerning memory capacity, Working Memory, complete Input-Output channel interaction. Volume 2 measures visual sequential, auditory and visual simultaneous short term memory with written responses; and auditory and visual simultaneous short term memory with verbal response thus allowing separate indices for inferior and superior temporal lobe functioning.

Interpretation of Volume 2 STM Derived Executive Processing Scores

2.4 and 2.5 Verbal STM

These variables are intended for comparison with VSTM as a bench mark There are no scaled scores for these variables. Instead use the relevant VSTM or ASTM for comparison. Assume the variables are the same unless the difference between the scaled scores exceeds the Minimum Significant Difference on the Scaled Score tables for the appropriate grade level.   Use the scaled scores for variables 2.16 and 2.17 for a more reliable estimate of visual/verbal stimulation effects or verbal/written response effects

2.7 Stimulus Complexity Ratio:

Stimulus complexity is a measure of the resistance to overload of the visual STM system. the score represents the relative memory for more complex words as opposed to simple letters. We have developed the stimulus complexity ratio by dividing the number of correct word responses in VSTM and VAPP by the number of correct letter responses in the same two tasks. Stimulus complexity scores are relatively independent of the overall quality or number of correct responses made in short term memory tasks, and must be interpreted in light of the total STM score. This ratio is multiplied by 100 to produce a percentage which is converted to normalized standard scores for interpretation. The median reliability of the Stimulus Complexity Ratio is: ($r_{tt.}$ =.86).

Interpreting Stimulus Complexity Scores
Lower scores signify a potential for stimulus overload with verbal materials. They indicate a lack of facility combining letters into words and generally show increasing difficulty with complex stimuli. Increasing the stimulus complexity markedly reduces the memory capacity of the learner for processing stimuli. Numerous causes may contribute to low STIMCOMP scores. Lack of automaticity or processing skill, a wide variety of temporary illness, anxiety and depression all may respond to treatment. Lack of capacity or developmental immaturity, neurogenic disorders may require compensations. Limited Stimulus complexity as with all short term memory measures is often symptomatic of dyslexia or other reading disorders. The clinician should adjust the curriculum stimulus load to the learners level of current ability and should design treatments with increasing stimulus complexity when a criterion of 80% is reached at the present teaching level.

2.8-2.9 Working Memory for letters and for
words is estimated from the efficiency of supra span of processing supra span items

Working Memory:
Working memory according to Baddeley (1990) is bounded

by the number of units to be processed, as well as the complexity of the processing. Each process, in Baddeley's terms has a response cost in reducing the number of stimulus items which can be handled. In the working memory literature there is an extreme variety of complex tasks with which various authors purport to measure working memory. It is difficult to determine what processes are actually involved or the amount of energy required, or the response cost of this plethora of unidentified processes. It is our position that working memory is not a unity but is a number of processes which may be applied to effect the response outcome depending upon the task and the stimulation. We propose enable the clinician to explore some of these working memory processes and to measure their response cost in the manner of Donders, (1863).

Initially, we are postulating that, for most individuals short term memory response to 3 or even 5 automatic stimuli requires no, or very little, processing and does not invoke "Working Memory". In essence 3 and often 5 simple letter or word stimuli are simply, in and out "knee jerk" responses. As the number of stimulus items increases and one exceeds this number of responses some increased processing is required to hold items long enough to repeat them.

We suggest that seven and nine stimuli meet or exceed the average processing requirement for adults, It is our assumption that as the limits of STM capacity are approached, the learner is required to institute a form of limited processing "holding" or rehearsal to maintain the stimuli while others are being presented. Theoretically this processing activates the prefrontal cortex. In essence we are suggesting that seven and nine stimuli usually require activation of the prefrontal cortex where as three and five do not. We are positing that the simple maintenance of a number of stimuli represents minimally complex processing and thus will serve as a stable baseline working memory. This baseline may be used for comparison when more complicated processes are invoked, to determine the response cost of the increased processing requirement.

Working memory as we have defined it includes presentation of greater than 5 stimuli for immediate recall. This procedure insures a standard processing requirement which is not too complex. To establish this stable working memory score we have summed the number of correct responses to 7 and 9 stimuli, by three modes of presentation, with written response, as our baseline working memory score. The sum of the correct responses for the seven and nine stimuli by the three stimulus modes is converted to normalized standard scores for interpretation. Since stimulus size is clearly a variable in memory the working memory index is calculated separately for letters and for words. Median reliability of the working memory for letters is r_{tt}. =.80 and for words is r_{tt}. =.82.

Interpreting Working Memory
Working memory is perhaps one of the most significant learning related variables available. Curricula which habitually overload the learner's working memory contribute significantly to many the reading and language handicaps. A cursory examination will give ample evidence of almost complete disdain for working memory or individual differences in most commercial curricula. The first tactic in therapeutic interventions is often adjustment of curriculum demands to the learner's working memory.

Dividing our working memory raw score by 6 will be an indication of an effective teaching memory unit size; when no additional processing is involved or no rehearsal is allowed. Knowledge of the magnitude of working memory gives an indication to clinicians, teachers and rehabilitation therapists of how much simple information the learner can easily handle with minimal processing at one item. These memory processing limitations will effect a learner's progress in reading, spelling, math, problem solving and nearly all areas of academic learning. The clinician should be alert that memory limitations in verbal processes, however, do not necessarily indicate limitations in mathematical or visual-pictorial memory. These and other areas of stimulation should be assessed independently. Note: the standard deviations for these scores are very large at the lower grades indicating a wide variation between learners.

2.7 Stimulus Complexity Ratio:

Stimulus complexity is a measure of the resistance to overload of the visual STM system. the score represents the relative memory for more complex words as opposed to simple letters. We have developed the stimulus complexity ratio by dividing the number of correct word responses in VSTM and VAPP by the number of correct letter responses in the same two tasks. Stimulus complexity scores are relatively independent of the overall quality or number of correct responses made in short term memory tasks, and must be interpreted in light of the total STM score. This ratio is multiplied by 100 to produce a percentage which is converted to normalized standard scores for interpretation. The median reliability of the Stimulus Complexity Ratio is: (r_{tt}. =.86).

TASK 14   5.5. STIMULUS COMPLEXITY RATIO
(STIMCOMP)

$$\frac{((\text{VSTM words} \underline{\hspace{1cm}} \text{ plus } \text{VAPP words}) + 1)\underline{\hspace{1cm}}}{((\text{VSTM letters} \underline{\hspace{1cm}} \text{ plus } \text{VAPP letters}) + 1) * 100 \underline{\hspace{1cm}}}$$ $\underline{\hspace{1cm}}$ $\underline{\hspace{1cm}}$

Interpreting Stimulus Complexity Scores
Lower scores signify a potential for stimulus overload with verbal materials. They indicate a lack of facility combining letters into words and generally show increasing difficulty with complex stimuli. Increasing the stimulus complexity

markedly reduces the memory capacity of the learner for processing stimuli. Numerous causes may contribute to low STIMCOMP scores. Lack of automaticity or processing skill, a wide variety of temporary illness, anxiety and depression all may respond to treatment. Lack of capacity or developmental immaturity, neurogenic disorders may require compensations. Limited Stimulus complexity as with all short term memory measures is often symptomatic of dyslexia or other reading disorders. The clinician should adjust the curriculum stimulus load to the learners level of current ability and should design treatments with increasing stimulus complexity when a criterion of 80% is reached at the present teaching level.

2.8-2.11 Working Memory for letters and for words is estimated from the efficiency of supra span of processing supra span items

Working Memory:
Working memory according to Baddeley (1990) is bounded by the number of units to be processed, as well as the complexity of the processing. Each process, in Baddeley's terms has a response cost in reducing the number of stimulus items which can be handled. In the working memory literature there is an extreme variety of complex tasks with which various authors purport to measure working memory. It is difficult to determine what processes are actually involved or the amount of energy required, or the response cost of this plethora of unidentified processes. It is our

position that working memory is not a unity but is a number of processes which may be applied to effect the response outcome depending upon the task and the stimulation. We propose enable the clinician to explore some of these working memory processes and to measure their response cost in the manner of Donders, (1863).

Initially, we are postulating that, for most individuals short term memory response to 3 or even 5 automatic stimuli requires no, or very little, processing and does not invoke "Working Memory". In essence 3 and often 5 simple letter or word stimuli are simply, in and out "knee jerk" responses. As the number of stimulus items increases and one exceeds this number of responses some increased processing is required to hold items long enough to repeat them.

We suggest that seven and nine stimuli meet or exceed the average processing requirement for adults, It is our assumption that as the limits of STM capacity are approached, the learner is required to institute a form of limited processing "holding" or rehearsal to maintain the stimuli while others are being presented. Theoretically this processing activates the prefrontal cortex. In essence we are suggesting that seven and nine stimuli usually require activation of the prefrontal cortex where as three and five do not. We are positing that the simple maintenance of a number of stimuli represents minimally complex processing and thus will serve as a stable baseline working memory. This baseline may be used for comparison when more complicated processes are invoked, to determine the response cost of the increased processing requirement.

Working memory as we have defined it includes presentation of greater than 5 stimuli for immediate recall. This procedure insures a standard processing requirement which is not too complex. To establish this stable working memory score we have summed the number of correct responses to 7 and 9 stimuli, by three modes of presentation, with written response, as our baseline working memory score. The sum of the correct responses for the seven and nine stimuli by the three stimulus modes is converted to normalized standard scores for interpretation. Since stimulus size is clearly a variable in memory the working memory index is calculated separately for letters and for words. Median reliability of the working memory indices for letters is r_{tt}. =.80 and for words is r_{tt}. =.82.

MEASURING Working Memory
The ability of the human mind to absorb and process information at one time is markedly limited. This limitation ranges from an estimated at 7 plus or minus 2, (Miller, 1952) units for adults confronted with overlearned stimuli, to 1 unit or perhaps less for youngsters with novel stimuli. When there is a requirement to process, combine or change the stimuli, the prefrontal cortex is activated (Goldman-Rakic, 1993) in prefrontal cortex)   and since the available energy or neural space is limited, this processing further reduces the number of units which may be apprehended. STM capacity varies from individual to individual and from task to task, and controls the overall rate of acquisition of knowledge, the amount of processing, and ultimately limits the complexity of the problem which may be solved.

The input and output processing of verbal material passes through the area surrounding the sylvian fissure between the orbital frontal cortex and the temporal lobe. A variety of Short Term memory tasks are designed to allow measurement of the functional efficiency of specific circuits of this Left Temporal Lobe and the Peri-Sylvian region. Administration time 15 minutes.

TASK 2.8. WORKING MEMORY, LETTERS (WKMEML)

(VSTM, 7+9 letters   ___

plus   ASTM, 7+9 letters   ___

plus

VAPP, 7+9 letters   ___ ___ ___

Interpreting Working Memory

Working memory is perhaps one of the most significant learning related variables available. Curricula which habitually overload the learner's working memory contribute significantly to many the reading and language handicaps. A cursory examination will give ample evidence of almost complete disdain for working memory or individual differences in most commercial curricula.

The first tactic in therapeutic interventions is often adjustment of curriculum demands to the learner's working memory.

Dividing our working memory raw score by 6 will be an indication of an effective teaching memory unit size; when no additional processing is involved or no rehearsal is allowed. Knowledge of the magnitude of working memory gives an indication to clinicians, teachers and rehabilitation therapists of how much simple information the learner can easily handle with minimal processing at one item. These memory processing limitations will effect a learner's progress in reading, spelling, math, problem solving and nearly all areas of academic learning. the clinician should be alert that memory limitations in verbal processes, however, do not necessarily indicate limitations in mathematical or visual-pictorial memory. These and other areas of stimulation should be assessed independently. Note: the standard deviations for these scores are very large at the lower grades indicating a wide variation between learners.

Table 2.1 Stimulus Overload

Working memory: average correct responses with 7 & 9 stimulus overload (N=1,920)

Variable	1	2	3	4	5	6	7/8	9/10	11+
		G R A D E							
Total Letters Recalled									
Mean letters recalled/48	14.9	20.3	25.3	28.1	30.7	32.8	32.2	34.5	38.9
Working STM Letters*	**2.5**	**3.5**	**4.0**	**4.5**	**5.0**	**5.5**	**5.5**	**5.5**	**6.5**
SD	6.3	8.0	6.8	5.4	6.6	6.8	8.6	6.5	5.1
Total Words Recalled									
Mean words recalled/48	3.9	8.3	14.0	15.6	19.2	20.2	19.9	22.0	24.8
Working STM Words*	**0.5**	**1.5**	**2.0**	**2.5**	**3.0**	**3.5**	**3.5**	**3.5**	**4.0**
SD	3.6	5.3	5.7	4.9	6.3	6.6	8.3	6.9	7.0

*

Rounded <u>down</u> to the nearest .5 to avoid overload.

It is important to note that the working memory for WORDS at first grade level is less than 1.0. Using whole words as teaching stimlui
generally exceeds the memory capacity of first grade learners. In general the effects of stimulus overload is greater as the complexity of the stimulus increases from letters to words.

TASK 2.9   57. WORKING MEMORY, WORDS (WKMEMW)

(VSTM, 7+9 words   ___
plus ASTM, 7+9 words   ___
plus VAPP, 7+9 words   ___

_____

Volume 2 also produces measures of impulsivity, working memory, stimulus complexity, surface sequencing, rehearsal, cross modal efficiency stimulus mode, response mode, and the interaction of stimulus number on sequencing. The five STM assessment tools will allow us to parse a number of other significant variables for school progress:

2.12 Impulsivity :

Individuals who tend to be impulsive often make a higher proportion of errors of commission.   In turn, written response STM tasks offer an accurate estimation of the number of errors of commission. We have developed a measure of impulsivity by the dividing the number of errors of commission in the three written response memory tasks to the number of correct responses on those same tasks. This ratio is multiplied by 100 to produce a percentage of error responses which is converted to normalized standard scores for interpretation. The median reliability of this variable is $r = .96$.

2.12. IMPULSIVITY (IMPULSE)

((VSTM errors   ___

plus ASTM errors   ___

plus VAPP errors+1)   ___ ___

divided by

(STM+1))*100   ___ ___

Errors of commission are an index of the individuals willingness to guess, to make random responses, or to take a chance on putting down a wrong answer to complete an exercise. Impulsivity is a measure of a tendency of the learner to make random responses under stress, or to rush to task completion regardless of the quality of the work. Fuster (1997) argues that impulse control is one of the functions of the prefrontal cortex, (in addition to working memory and preparatory set, and is necessary temporal organization and sequencing of language. Among other functions, the prefrontal cortex, in particular the orbito-frontal area is responsible for inhibition. Impulsivity, the lack of inhibition may indicates ineffective functioning of the orbito-frontal cortex. (Loge, Staton, & Beatty, 1990), and has been related to borderline personality disorder (Lumsden,

1993).This particular circuit has been implicated in Attention Deficit Disorder, (Barkley, 1992), Impulsivity has been shown to be common in children with several disorders; children with Attention Deficit Disorder, (August, & Garfinkel, 1990; Korkman, & Pesonen, 1994; & Kupietz, 1990); Learning Disability, (Korkman, & Pesonen, 1994). Reading Disability, (August, & Garfinkel, 1990; Kupietz, 1990); and Turner's Syndrome, (Williams, et. Al., 1991).

Impulsivity interacts with anxiety and extroversion (Pliszka, 1990; and Revelle, 1987) (Wilding, 1984), and has been linked to a serotonin imbalance, (Lawlor, 1990; and Zubieta, & Alessi, 1993). Stimulants such as Caffeine tend to induce impulsivity, (Anderson, & Revelle, 1983). and it is more common in children exposed prenatally to marijuana, cigarettes, and alcohol (Fried, Watkinson, & Gray, 1992).

Revelle, (1987) noted some similarities and differences between impulsivity and anxiety in the manner in which they interfere with memory. The impulsive child is more likely to trade-off speed for accuracy. The neurotic child more likely to emphasize accuracy. The impulsive child is less likely to be persistent than the anxious child and may have attention problems.

On the other hand, individuals who respond to methylphenidate, have been found to be less impulsive (de-Sonneville, et. al., 1994). In addition, Conners, et al, (1996) in a double blind trial with ADHD children, found Bupropion may was effective in controlling impulsivity, conduct disorder and hyperactivity in children, and may act as an alternative to methylphenidate.

TBI and Head Injury and Impulsivity

Impulsive symptoms consistent with dysfunction of the frontal lobes can occur following traumatic brain injury (TBI) or other types of acquired brain injury (stroke, aneurysm). These symptoms can include problems with short-term memory, attention, planning, problem solving, impulsivity, disinhibition, poor motivation, and other behavioral and cognitive deficits ("frontal lobe syndrome"). Kraus, & Maki, (1997) used a dopaminergic agent (amantadine) showed positive results with TBI patients.

Testosterone and impulsivity

Of interest to the school neuropsychologist dealing with adolescent boys, Bjork, et. al., (2001) using a version of a continuous performance test and testosterone levels with individuals with real-world aggressive histories and self-reported impulsivity have correlated with commission errors (failures to withhold responses to non-target stimuli) in versions of the continuous performance test (CPT) the results of this study support a positive relationship between testosterone and impulsivity.

Alcohol and increased impulsivity

Dougherty, el al., (1999) report commission errors measured during peak breath alcohol concentrations on a delayed memory task were significantly correlated with scores on the Barratt Impulsivity Scale. Immediate memory tasks showed no effect from the alcohol. Expanding the same research theme, Dougherty, et al., (2000) found alcohol related to inattention, impulsivity, discrimination, and response criteria when a variety of dependent measures are used.

Interpreting Impulsivity Scores

Impulsivity is estimated from the ratio of errors of

commission to correct responses in STM written response tasks. A high Impulsivity score indicates an individual who is prone to guess at answers, who may be compliant to surface task demands, often in the learning situations where task completion, or time on task rather than task quality is emphasized. A high score on this variable is not limited to, but, not unusual in delinquent populations and is an indicator of confabulation. It is not unusual to find that learners, who have their memories overloaded, guess, or respond to faint memory traces. Generally individuals who indulge in mild guessing perform better, not only on the memory tasks but in academics as well.

A low score on the impulsivity variable indicates a compliant learner who tends to become over-cautious and anxious when insecure in academic tasks. This learner generally is afraid of making a mistake and a low score is often indicative of high levels of repression or inhibition. This is often expressed as a perfectionist tendency where the individual cannot reveal any flaws and at the same time must inspect everything to find the most minute irregularity. Generally this is enhanced by an over-controlling environment, although scores on this variable often reflect basic personality structures. At the extreme this score may indicate a tendency toward obsessive compulsivity.

2.13 Rehearsal :

Rehearsal is the oldest and most effective formalized cognitive processing algorithm. The one working memory "process" which Baddeley has clearly identified is Rehearsal, (Baddeley, 1978, Baddeley & Hitch, 1974). Baddeley sees rehearsal as the process whereby verbal materials are "kept alive" in STM. This is subject to the restriction of short term memory span of course. By repeating words in one's head, verbal material can be kept in working memory almost indefinitely (Baddeley, 1986). Within this Articulatory Loop, verbal stimuli will remain, intact, as long as they are rehearsed, but the information dissipates rapidly when the looping stops, Our measures of Short Term Memory allow us to develop an estimate of the learners skill at rehearsal.

Rehearsal vs. Repetition

To begin with the school neuropsychologist needs to differentiate between two similar concepts repetition and rehearsal. Repetition is repeating something a number of times while rehearsal is reviewing things with an intent to learn. It is this "intent to learn" is an active proces while rehearsal is passive It is active versus passive processing that makes the difference between these two concepts. These concepts are rarely differentiated in practice and most teachers assume the child is repeating the material with the intent to learn and are often surprised when the child "forgets" material he has repeated numerous times. Rehearsal appears to be an independent process from memory. Ronnberg, et al., (1996) studied cases of mild aphasia resulting from subarachnoid hemorrhage and found that the phonological loop and the central executive aspects of working memory were impaired and dissociable from the rehearsal process which was unaffected

The two concepts are often confused in the literature as well as in education. Repetition seems to activate the posterior brain Intention to learn the distinguishing mark of rehearsal, Intention to learn as we recall from Volume two activates the dorsolateral prefrontal cortex to a much greater extent than does repetition

As an example of the differentiation between repetition and rehearsal, Cornette, et al., (2001) used P.E.T. on two different type tasks. The first task required a quick decision on stimulus orientation and did not maintain the stimulus. Whereas in the second task the learner was required to maintain the information during the presentation of a second stimulus required maintenance in storage and rehearsal. Differences in the areas of the brain which were activated were striking. The short repetition task activated a large expanse of occipito-temporal cortex with a difference in activation dependent upon the rate of presentation of the stimuli: A fast trial rate engaged posterior regions, a slow trial rate anterior regions. For the more complex rehearsal task, working memory for orientation, the left inferior parietal cortex, left dorsolateral prefrontal cortex and a left superior frontal sulcus region, and to a lesser degree the symmetrical right superior frontal region and a left superior
parietal region were activated

Measuring Rehearsal Effects
We have measured rehearsal strategy efficiency by developing a ratio correct responses between VSTM, successive presentation, and VAPP, simultaneous presentation, which does not. The presentation rate of one stimulus every two seconds in the VSTM task allows time for rehearsal. The simultaneous presentation of the stimulus groups in the VAPP task does not afford rehearsal time and requires responding from memory traces in the "Iconic Store". The ratio developed by dividing the correct responses in the VSTM task by the responses in the VAPP task reflects the relative effectiveness of these two presentation modes and allows us to infer rehearsal effectiveness. This ratio is converted to normalized standard scores for interpretation.

The Median reliability for Rehearsal is r.=.90.

TASK 2.13   59. REHEARSAL EFFECTS (REHEARSE)

((VSTM TOTAL+1)   ___
divided by
(VAPP TOTAL+1))*100   ___   _____ _____

Interpreting Rehearsal Scores

A low score indicates an individual who is less effective when allowed time for rehearsal than when confronted with simultaneous presentation. This may be seen as related to poor rehearsal strategy, to lack of development of a rehearsal strategy, or to interference from other stimulation such as noise, anxiety, or depression.

A high score indicates an individual who profits from the additional time afforded by the 2 second presentation time in VSTM. Indications are that this time is spent effectively and the inference that effective rehearsal has transpired. This usually indicated an effective learner, although it is possible to over-rehearse. Buckalew and Hickey (1984) found an exposure duration phenomenon which they termed 'span of apprehension, an analogue of the VAPP simultaneous presentation phenomenon and suggests that anxious persons are more likely to attempt to 'read' simultaneously presented materials item by item, instead of the more efficient 'coup d'oeil' or taking it in with a glance. Thus when one is presenting the VAPP or the VSTM stimuli observations that the learner is attempting to reading item by item or attempting to rehearse during VAPP are indicators of anxiety.

Observation of the learner during these tasks is critical for interpretation. Rehearsal attempts and sequences can be directly observed by watching lip movements in some learners. Use of place markers or numeration as aids is usually obvious and is counterproductive

It should be remembered when interpreting this score that it is not independent of the initial VSTM and VAPP scores A high rehearsal score developed from low memory scores does not reflect good rehearsal, but rather, poorer employment of the Iconic Store in visual apprehension. This is a rehearsal efficiency score and suggests to the examiner where rehearsal may be a source of learning difficulty. the actual procedure used by the learner should be explored through observation and focused questioning.

Rehearsal is an important measure of the internal processing of material in short term memory. We are not here, concerned with the nature of the process, but rather the effectiveness of whatever process the learner is using. If deficiency is found, further exploration into the nature of the process is warranted.

Treatment of rehearsal inefficiency usually involves establishing a simple effective learning routine, demonstrating its effectiveness to the learner and monitoring usually for several months gradually fading the frequency of monitoring as the strategy proves routine.

Rehearsal in the classroom
This difference between rehearsal and repetition can be clearly seen, in several instances. Repetition tends to occur during such teacher directed activities such as choral speaking; where the stimulus is present during the response;

or where the response is not obvious. The child who writes on the chalkboard "I will not chew gum" is engaging in repetition, but is unlikely to include the intention to allow the phrase to become a permanent process. It is not that such repetitions cannot result in learning, but they are entirely dependent upon the learner intent to learn,. Although the learner may invoke "intent" more or less at will, for the teacher rehearsal is insured only when the stimulus is removed and the response is obvious and the child had to formulate the response him or herself.

As a method of learning, rehearsal has been found to be more effective than the Key Word method (Gupta, & Dash, (1989), (Wang, et al., 1993) or than strategy training, or attribution methods of learning foreign languages (Turner, Dofny, Dutka, 1994). However, rehearsal and attribution, was the most effective. Similarly, Wang, (1990) found 2nd graders who chose elaboration, (rehearsing and relating to known material), learned 3 times more material than Ss who preferred simple rote rehearsal. On the other hand Wood, Willoughby, Bolger, Younger, et-al., (1993) while confirming Wang's (1990) results with bright students found the repetition with elaboration method was no different from simple repetition for low achievers, probably since elaboration requires greater working memory. While rehearsal alone is more effective than most single learning methods, rehearsal combined with some form of "depth" processing seems to be even more effective. Spacing rehearsals enhances the effect on learning and on long term memory (Greene, 1990; and Wright, Cook, Rivera, Shyan, et al., 1990).

First grade children usually do not understand about the

effectiveness of rehearsal for memory, or the comprehension-memory strategy distinction, but normal development of this and other learning processes continues at least through junior high school (Henry, & Millar, 1993; and Lovett, & Flavell, 1991). Henry, (1991), found children from age 5 to 9 profited from the rehearsal training to a similar extent. On the other hand, Douglas, & Benezra, (1990) found ADHD boys to be deficit in rehearsal, organization, and sustained strategic effort, and careful consideration of response alternatives. This pattern suggests impaired self-regulatory or "executive" processes. Reading disabled boys had more deficits in verbal processing and STM. LD boys are suspected of being deficient in Visual rehearsal, (Peynircioglu, 1995) but not in non-verbal recognition memory (Santiago, & Matos, 1994).

Repetition and Satiation
Repetition and rehearsal however induce another phenomenon, satiation which results in a loss of learning effectiveness and boredom. Satiation can be readily induced in less than 15 seconds by repeating a word or phrase rapidly as possible over and over again, First to deteriorate is the timing or rhythm of pronunciation where suddenly the end of the phrase becomes the beginning and the utterance, to the outside observer becomes gibberish. Shortly after this rhythm shift the meaning begins to disintegrate as well. We may deduce that the access to the stored meaning is dependent upon the rhythm of the phoneme chain that activates it and when one changes the phoneme chain, as occurs in satiation, it no longer activates the same meaning, recovery from satiation is automatic, but it is easier to induce for the same combination in the future. This phenomenon occurred to me as a child learning the alphabet Satiation was responsible for

my thinking that "elemenoh" was a word and wondering what it meant up through most of my second grade career. It was disappointing when I finally worked out that it was really L, M, N, O in the alphabet Satiation is one reason that spacing repetitive and spacing stimuli trials has always been found to be is more effective than high rate massed trials in learning Spacing rehearsal over time helps prevent this satiation effect as does application of the material in differing contexts

Neuro-imaging evidence
This subvocal rehearsal localizes the distribution of regional cerebral blood flow (rCBF) to the left supramarginal gyrus, for phonological materials and sub-vocal rehearsal with Broca's area. (Paulesu, Frith, & Frackowiak, 1993) The Neural circuitry for rehearsal is not clearly established but it is likely that the Secondary Motor Area on the medial side of motor planning area (Brodmann's area 6), (Roland, et-al., 1977) is involved in addition to the auditory-verbal neural route.

The processing of visual material in Short Term Memory uses different neural pathways. Talon-Bawdry, Bertrand, & Filcher, (2001) using human intracranial recordings found that limited regions of extra striate visual associative areas, separated by several centimeters, become synchronized in an oscillatory mode during the rehearsal (subvocal Imagery repetition) of an object in visual short-term memory.

Fez, et-al., (1996) presented verbal word and pseudoword stimuli for 40 second rehearsal and found increases were found bilaterally in the dorsolateral prefrontal cortex and cerebellum, and medially in the supplementary motor area. They posit that the dorsolateral prefrontal cortical areas contribute to the maintenance of both verbal and nonverbal information, whereas left frontal opercular regions appear to be involved specifically in the rehearsal of verbal material. The parietal cortex which is involved in encoding and decoding verbal stimuli is not activated by rehearsal. Jonides, et al., (1998) found by isolating the several components of verbal working memory that the retrieval aspect of the memory reliably engaged the dorsolateral prefrontal, anterior cingulate, posterior parietal, and extra striate cortices

Rehearsal can compensate to a limited degree for severe Korsakoff-type amnesia. (Goldstein, & Malec, 1989) (Weingartner, et-al., 1993), who also found persons with Alzheimer's Dementia do not seem to profit from rehearsal. Depressed boys ages 9-11 rehearsed less and when they did had a smaller rehearsal set size, (Osborn, & Meador, 1989). Depressed adults also had shorter length of the rehearsal loop. (Channon, Baker, & Robertson, 1993). However when exposed to repetitions of words, depressed patients profited more than normals, Alzheimer's or Korsakoff's (Weingartner, et-al., 1993).

2.14-2.16 Stimulus-response modality

Learners skills with input media and output media are not always the same, generally a visual stimulus leads to a written response whereas an auditory stimulus is most effective with a verbal response. This section allows us to explore the ability of the learner to respond to Visual versus Auditory stimulation; Verbal versus written response; and the effectiveness of cross modal responding.

2.15 Cross-modal Comparison

Cross modal responding is returning a response in a medium

other than the presentation mode. This verbal imitation and copying are unimodal whereas spelling and reading aloud are cross modal. whether by design or by habituation, unimodal responding is generally more facile. Cross-modal responding is clearly neurologically more complicated requiring the translation from one symbol system to another. Our memory tasks VSTM, VAPP, and AVSTM are all unimodal in that the learner produces a written response for a visual stimulus or a verbal response to an auditory stimulus. On the other hand ASTM and VVAPP are cross-modal. We have developed our measure by summing the ASTM and VVAPP raw scores and dividing by the sum of the VAPP and the AVSTM scores. This resulting ratio is controlled for stimulus presentation type and response mode as well as rehearsal effects. The ratio multiplied by 100 to generate a percent and is converted to normalized standard scores for interpretation. The median reliability of the Cross-Modal index is r.=.85.

Interpretation
A high score suggests that cross-modal responding is more effective than unimodal responding. Lower scores indicate an advantage for uni-modal responding.

Note: The present standard score table is developed from the ratio of ASTM and VAPP alone since there is not presently sufficient data from AVSTM and VVAPP.

TASK 20   CROSS MODAL EFFICIENCY (CROSMODE)

             ((ASTM TOTAL   ___
      plus   VVAPP TOTAL+1)   ___
      divided by
             (AVSTM TOTAL   ___
      plus   VSTM TOTAL+1))*100   ___

2.16 Stimulus Mode :

The Stimulus Mode measure is a comparison of the learner's relative effectiveness with visual versus auditory stimuli. We have developed this measure by summing ASTM with AVSTM and dividing by the sum of VAPP and VSTM.   This effectively reduces the influence of the response mode and isolates processing of the neural circuit including the superior temporal gyrus form processing in the occipital lobe and the inferior temporal gyrus. The resulting ratio is multiplied by 100 to produce a percentage and converted to normalized standard scores for interpretation. Present median reliability for the stimulus mode comparison is, r. =.96.

Very few individuals are completely lacking in one or another of these skills.   The score we have devised reflects the relative efficiency of these modes of presentation.   These ratios, as with most, must be interpreted in relation to the basic ability level reflected in the standard score for VSTM and VAPP. Our initial concept in developing the AVSTM task was that stimulus mode should have the greatest significance in primary school years. Accordingly we developed standardization data for grades 1 to 3 only. Thus, as of this writing there is sufficient data for this formula for standardization from grade 1 through grade 3. Above grade three the present Stimulus Mode standard scores were developed from the ratio of ASTM and VSTM.

The scoring is designed so a <u>high</u> score reflects an advantage for <u>auditory</u>, superior temporal gyrus, presentation channels. The <u>low</u> score represents increased benefit for <u>visual</u>, inferior temporal lobe, efficiency.

In designing treatments, a high score should not be construed to limit presentations to the auditory channel, but may indicate that the visual channel needs more emphasis, or more careful stimulus selection, to increase facility with the interpretation of visual materials.

TASK 2.16 STIMULUS MODE (STIMMODE)
            ((ASTM TOTAL   ___
    plus   AVSTM TOTAL+1)   ___
    divided by
            (VSTM TOTAL   ___
    plus VVAPP TOTAL+1))*100 ___ ___ ___

2.17 Response Mode :
The response mode measure is designed to describe the relationship of oral and written responses. In the early grades oral responses take a definite preference over written responding, but as skill in written responses increases this relationship becomes more balanced but, rarely equal. The sum of Both AVSTM and VVAPP gives us an index of oral responding, while ASTM plus VAPP is a measure of written responding. The ratio thus formed is controlled for stimulus type and rehearsal effects and reflects the relative skill at oral and written responding. The resultant ratio is an indicator of

the relative efficiency of the neural circuits connecting Broca's area with the "motor - mouth" or with the "motor - hand" sections of Brodmann's area 4. This ratio is multiplied by 100 to produce a percentage and converted to normalized standard scores for interpretation. The present reliability for response mode comparisons is, r.=.94.

As of this writing, there is insufficient data for the VVAPP task to develop adequate norms, and the AVSTM data is limited to grades 1-3. as a result the present norms are developed above grades 1-3 using AVSTM and ASTM only.

Since our experience with most of these ratios indicates little significance in change in these relationships at the upper grades, we have reported the grade 3 standard scores for all grades above there. These data should be interpreted with caution pending more definitive results.

Interpreting Response Mode Scores
A high scaled score indicates a relative facility with oral responses. A low score indicates a relative advantage for written response. As with the previous measure this should not necessarily be construed as limiting responses to the preferred mode, but may indicate the necessity for instruction and curriculum modification in the less efficient modality.

TASK 2.17 RESPONSE MODE (RESPMODE)
            ((AVSTM TOTAL   ___
      plus   VVAPP TOTAL+1)   ___
      divided by

$$ \text{plus} \quad \frac{\text{ASTM TOTAL}}{\text{VAPP TOTAL}+1))*100} \underline{\quad\quad} $$

In general with a learner who can read visual stimuli are more effective for learning than auditory stimuli. Similarly a written response is more effective for learning than an verbal response. A part of this is due to the stability of the stimulation. A visual stimulus may be consulted and inspected several times whereas an auditory stimulus in fleeting, and is dependent upon the articulatory loop. Similarly a written response involves a greater number of neural systems and hence activates a greater portion of the learner.

Auditory stimulation is effective with individuals who cannot read, unfortunately auditory stimuli are a step removed from reality and thus more likely to be vague, but is most effective for rehearsal of material that is already learned

2.18- 2.20. Short Term Memory Sequencing

Sequencing is the return of stimuli from short term memory in the order in which they are presented. As such measures of sequencing assess the ability to return items in a STM Capacity measure but to maintain control of the sequence of items as well Sequencing is a two edged sword. Too little sequencing reflects a disordered or distorted input and may effectively distort perception, of events. Too much sequencing tends to interfere with STM and individuals may persevere on the order, rather than the content. Sequencing is a DLPFC function beyond simple supra-span immediate memory.

Scoring Sequencing :

There are several ways of scoring for sequencing or seriation. The method we have developed depends upon specific sequencing of any two words in presentation order. Thus:

1. If the first word in the response list is the same as the first word in the presentation list this receives a sequencing score of 1.

2. If the second word follows a correct first word and is the same as the second word in the presentation it receives a sequencing score of 1.

3. If any other word directly follows the word that preceded it in the stimulus presentation list it is given a score of 1.

4. The total number of sequenced items for each the STM list are summed and, the scores are placed on the Student Record form for each Short-Term Memory Process

Sequencing is the total proportion of the responses made in presentation order in the three Short Term Memory written response tasks. We have limited this variable to written tasks because the reliability of scoring sequencing in oral responses is somewhat lower. The Sequencing score is a ratio score of the total number of responses made in correct sequence divided by the sum of correct responses on the VSTM, ASTM and VAPP tasks for both letters and words. This ratio is multiplied by 100 to generate a percentage, and converted to normalized standard scores for interpretation. The median reliability of Sequencing is r_{tt}. =.89.

TASK 2.18 MEMORY RESPONSE SEQUENCING (MEMSEQ)

              ((VSTM, SEQ TOTAL ___
    pus   ASTM, SEQ TOTAL ___
    plus   VAPP, SEQ TOTAL+1) ___
             divided by
     (STM TOTAL+1))*100   ___ ___ ___

Interpretation of Sequencing Scores :
Limited Sequencing suggests a disruption in processing the input of stimuli In turn this suggests the learner may have a distorted picture of the stimulus array, which may in turn result in disorganization. The sequencing process is perhaps most clearly seen in spelling, which depends upon, not only responding with the correct letters but also presenting them in a correct sequence. Sequencing faults are responsible for a large proportion of spelling errors as witness a spelling demon like "receive". Sequencing is a bivariate variable and extreme scores in either direction may be significant. A high score indicates an individual who is likely to sequence responses. This sequencing seems to assist in remembering at some level but for some learner's as the sequencing increases it takes precedence over the items to be remembered and the memory span is reduced by the additional processing and may reflect an individual whose need for order interferes with the learning of the content. It is not uncommon to see a learner's memory blocked for want of the next item in the sequence.   Extreme high scores on this variable may be characteristic of individuals with compulsive or obsessive tendencies. Such learners are often

compulsive in other areas of responding as well. This need for order generally interferes with acquisition of new learning, but may be helpful in retrieval of already learned materials.

A low score indicates an individual who does not return responses in presentation order is characteristically made by an individual with a tendency toward disorder. Low sequencing may indicate some interference in STM processing. Sequencing often generalizes to other areas and these individuals often have difficulty with sequencing and organization of many life tasks. Similarly they may be poor learners because of overload and difficulty in retrieval of information. Sequencing is amenable to treatment. Clinically, we have found that sequencing generalizes across tasks and training in sequencing transfers to other situations including organizing school work.

Sequencing as an independent Process
Sequencing is a frontal lobe processing function that serves the purpose of organization and is a critical problem solving skill. As such the sequencing process is independent of neural channel, Pickering, Gathercole, & Peaker, 1998) content (Avons, 1998) or memory (Parmentier, & Jones, 2000) . Studies with fMRI (Henson, Burgess, & Frith, 2000) studying immediate recall of visual short term memory have shown activation of the left dorsolateral premotor cortex is involved in the maintenance of temporal order, possibly as the location of a timing signal used in the rhythmic organization of rehearsal, while memory for words seems to activate verbal item information in left posterior temporal areas and short-term storage of phonological information in left supra-marginal gyrus (Pecan, Levy, Police, Crozier, Lehericy, Pillon, Deweer, Le-Bihan, & Dubois, 2001). Broca's area supports the articulatory processes required for phonological recoding

of visual stimuli (Henson, Burgess, & Frith, 2000).

Sequencing vs. Seriation

As an independent process sequencing can act either as an enhancement to memory as for example the syntactic sequence in a sentence affords greater recall of words than random placement. Sequencing may also act as a deterrent to short term memory if the sequencing is blocked in the middle and the individual does not have sufficient flexibility to sidestep the sequence in favor of recalling recency items. This Blockage dependent upon not being able to recall sequence is more common in anxious individuals.

An illustration of this independence of sequencing is found in an in depth analysis of a single case study where memory itself appeared to be normal, the ability to sequence was deficit. Romani, Ward, & Olson, (1999) found their subject performed poorly in tasks that involve detection of the order of adjacent letters in a word or the order of adjacent units in strings of consonants or symbols. Finally, he performs poorly in tasks that involve reconstructing the order of a series of complex visual characters. They argue This may have resulted in a holistic word-based reading strategy, which, together with the original problem of encoding order, may have had detrimental effects for the acquisition of spelling.

Sequencing is positional not temporal

While much initial thinking about sequencing saw it as a manifestation of time that is it was the temporal order of the stimuli which determined a sequence. In contrast, Henson, (1998) Agues, that of the three solutions to the problem of serial order, chaining, ordinal and positional theories. Error patterns in serial recall from short-term memory fail to support chaining theories, yet provide unequivocal evidence for positional theories. Henson (1998) proposes a Start-End Model (SEM), wherein the positions of items in a sequence are coded relative to both the start and end of that sequence Unlike other positional models however, SEM predicts that positional errors will maintain relative rather than absolute position. Evidence suggests that short-term memory for serial order includes information about the positions of items in a sequence. This information is necessary to explain why substitution errors between sequences tend to maintain their position within a sequence. Using sequences of differing lengths Henson, (1999) found the position of intrusions were relative to both the beginning and the end points of the sequence.

Sequencing and seriation are different processes
It is necessary to differentiate the sequencing measure in short term memory from the Seriation measure in Volume 2 Learning and Retention Processes. We have chosen to apply the term Sequencing to returning stimuli in short term memory tasks in the presentation order. Sequencing usually occurs without intervention of the learner and thus is primarily memory traces from activation of the neurons in the temporal lobe. Thus, sequencing is expected to last as long as that activation lasts. Excessive emphasis on sequencing as a process can be inhibitory because it occupies some of the energy that might otherwise be devoted to item recall.

We will differentiate between measures of short term memory sequencing (returning stimuli in presentation sequence from immediate memory without processing) and seriation (retrieving stimuli in a reconstructed presentation order after time and or processing). Longer term memory requires reformulating the sequence as well as recall of the individual items. Wildgruber, et al, (1999) employed fMRI in

normal subjects to study reversal of an automatic sequence
As compared to the response obtained during forward
recitation, re-sequencing of the word string yielded additional
activation of the bilateral middle and inferior frontal gyri, the
posterior parietal cortex and the left anterior cingulate gyrus.
This activation diminished with repetition. We will deal with
seriation more intensively in Volume 7.

Seriation is retrieval of acquired information in some
presentation sequence. Seriation is reserved for returning
stored responses retrieved from memory in some order, not
necessarily presentation order. Seriation requires some
processing to sequence the responses whether in
presentation order, alphabetical order, order of magnitude.
Acquired information is not necessarily stored in an order or a
sequence. Seriation requires the application of some
sequencing principle, perhaps stored in the basal ganglia to a
group of disordered stimuli to develop a meaningfully
organized response array. As an organizational principle it
may effect to increase recall by indicating a relationship with
the succeeding responses. Seriation then is organizing stimuli
on the response side while sequencing is recalling the order
of stimulation. The correlation between these two measures
is r. = .34. Indicating that, although the method of
calculation is identical but the circumstances differ, there is
very little relationship between the two measures which share
only 12% joint variance.

Sequencing ability or the ability to organize grammatical
sequences is spared in hippocampal lesions and can be
considered implicit memory, or process learning (Cleermans,
1993) Studies with rats, have shown that ablation of specific
nerves in the striatum will prevent the sequencing of
grooming behavior in the rat. This suggests that the

sequencing process is very primitive, developed early and is in part embedded in the basal ganglia and the limbic system. Sequencing ability then appears to be implicit learning or process learning and may occur automatically without awareness.   Hartman, Knopman, & Nissen, (1989). demonstrated that learning of a repeating sequence of verbal stimuli occurred without awareness, but only when the stimulus-response mapping required an attention-demanding activity (i.e. categorizing the stimuli): subjects also showed implicit sequence learning when the task involved either motor responses to verbal stimuli or verbal responses to spatially arranged stimuli.

Sequencing and Handicaps :
The relationship of Sequencing to various disorders is complex where sequencing is effected by some disorders and not by others.   Bell, (1990) for instance found 11-14 yr old dyslexics are not deficient in rapid sequencing in STM. however, sequencing difficulties in dyslexics were reported by Evans, Drasdo, & Richards, (1994), and (Singleton, 1988). For learners with LD the picture is somewhat different. If spelling was the only presenting problem, LD's were found deficient in sequencing in visual STM. On the other hand, Batchelor, et al, (1990) reported that when the presenting problem was reading the cognitive processing deficits are much more complex.   Oberklaid, Harris, Keir, (1989) found strong correlations between both parental and teacher ratings of a child's language problem, teacher rating of reading and sequencing problems, short term auditory memory and neurodevelopmental finding of auditory sequencing problems. Plenkovic, (1988). reports autistic Ss performed significantly worse on visual sequential memory subtests, but not the auditory. Sequencing is also effected in deaf children, (Wallace, & Corballis, 1973); Multiple Sclerosis (Grigsby, et al,

1994); and Aphasia, (Gutbrod, et al, 1989) and Wold, &
Reinvang, 1990).

Kiefer, (1989) reports a case study of an 8 year old with
difficulty with attention, sequencing and short term memory
which was ascribed to anxiety .

Anxiety, Depression and Short Term Memory

There are two ways to look a the interaction of STM and
anxiety, opposite sides of the same coin. Torgensen (1982)
indicates two basic sources for STM deficits in children with
learning disabilities. The first of these is problems with
control processes such as anxiety, impulsivity and attention.
Here the emotion itself acts to inhibit learning. The second
source for STM deficits is structural, the capacity of the
individual to process information. In this instance it is the
task itself that interferes with learning and may also be the
cause of the emotional response leading to further
suppression.

While the phenomenon of anxiety induced by stimulus
overload is common knowledge, most of the research follows
Torgensons first model where pre-existing anxiety is shown
to effect STM or learning. Relatively little is known about
STM overload induced anxiety, which may be a greater
problem for school children who have less choice in avoiding
overload stimulation and fewer mental processing skills to
deal with it.

Eysenck, & Calvo, (1992) elaborating upon Eysencks
(1979) theory relating anxiety to processing efficiency in
memory, argue that anxiety causes worry (ie a verbal
manifestation of anxiety), and worry impairs performance on

tasks with high attentional or short-term memory demands. Anxiety may not effect memory span for simple items or where the processing requirement is minimal. A paper by Boulenger, et al, (1988) makes a similar point. In their view the anxiety tends to focus the individuals attention on subjective danger which in turn impact on memory and concentration. Additional support for the Eysenck position is found in the work of MacLeod, & Donnellan, (1993) who found disproportionately long latencies for high anxious individuals on complex tasks, when compared with low anxious on high and low memory load grammatical reasoning tasks, indicating that anxiety is more likely to effect processing than capacity.

The findings for depressed patients are somewhat different, In general depressed patients respond more slowly, attributed to motivation, not response speed, Abas, Sahakian, & Levy, (1990). The depressed patient's STM is effected compared with normal controls but they are not as compromised as patients with dementia, (Whall, 1986) or Alzhiemers, (Dannenbaum, & Parkinson, 1988).

Verbalization, Memory, and Anxiety
While anxiety interferes with STM, this interference is restricted to the verbal materials. Sullivan, et al, (1986) using a variety of memory tasks on Alzheimer's patients concluded that the verbal and non verbal memory systems can deteriorate independently. Caplan, et al, (1986) report similar verbal STM deficit after left hemisphere infarct, but S's short term memory was good on tasks (pointing and recognition) that did not require verbal output. Markham, & Darke, (1991) tested high and low anxious college students on verbal and spatial memory tasks. They found an anxiety effect only for complex verbal tasks supporting the Eysenck

position and indicating that anxiety effects memory only in the verbal channel. This restriction of the effects of anxiety to the verbal realm was supported by Rapee, (1993) who found that generation of random letters was the only task of several which inhibited induced worry. He concluded that worry uses primarily the phonological aspect of working memory. Visuo-spatial tasks did not interfere with worry.

ADHD and Language problems and sequencing

In a group of ADHD youngsters, Tirosh, & Cohen, (1998) found a 45% rate of language problems. This comorbidity is more prevalent among girls (P = .02). Both sequencing and short-term memory were significantly related to attention-deficit with language problems, but the attention scores were not. This suggests a different etiology for children with ADHD combined with language problems. Cousens, et al, (1991) report that sequencing ability, along with short term memory, distractibility, and attention are negatively effected by central nervous system prophylaxis for acute lymphoblastic leukemia, and by radiation treatment for brain tumors (Dennis, et-al., 1992);

Memory and the Elderly

Traditionally memory is considered to deteriorate with age. Salthouse, (1990) reviewed the literature relating to memory and ageing, and found studies using formalized assessment approaches consistently found a reduction in short term memory functioning with age. In later studies, Salthouse, (1992), and Salthouse, & Skovronek, (1992) found the temporary memory for of untransformed stimulus information to be preserved in elderly subjects, but the deficiency was found in the processing the information in working memory. A similar finding comparing STM with "Secondary memory" was reported by Delbecq-Derouesne, & Beauvois, (1989).

With elderly persons, sequencing in tasks like remembering phone number sequences to dial them becomes increasingly difficult, (West, & Crook, 1991). Seriation, the application of established orders or sequences does not seem to dissipate so rapidly. Wiegersma, & Meertse, (1990) found performance in 63-69 year olds declined significantly with age on tasks, requiring generating a subjective order of a sequence of responses, but not in tasks, which involve reproduction of a presented sequence. In essence the process of sequencing stimuli deteriorates with age to a greater extent than item recall in STM.

 It should be noted that each of these handicapping conditions also tends to restrict STM capacity and difficulties with sequencing may result from limited storage capacity which is more readily overloaded and interferes with sequencing processing.

2.19 Working Memory Sequencing Ratio

This measure is an index of the competition of working memory processing with sequencing. The Working Memory scoring of the STM tasks requires the additional processing of holding or rehearsing in memory. The Working Memory Sequencing Ratio is designed to demonstrate the effects of this additional processing on sequencing. Working Memory Sequencing is calculated the number of items returned in presentation sequence for 7 and 9 word stimuli on the VSTM, ASTM, and the VAPP tasks divided by the number of correct responses for the same items on those tasks, to control for memory skill and isolate the sequencing factor. The resulting proportion is multiplied by 100 to produce a percentage which is converted to a normalized standard score for interpretation. The median reliability for working memory sequencing is, r. =.92.

TASK 2.19 WORKING MEMORY SEQUENCING (WKMEMSEQ)
$$((VSTM, SEQ\ 7+9\ WORD \quad \underline{\quad}$$
$$plus\ ASTM, SEQ\ 7+9\ WORDS \quad \underline{\quad}$$
$$plus\ VAPP, SEQ\ 7+9\ WORDS+1) \quad \underline{\quad} \quad \underline{\quad}$$
$$divided\ by$$

$$(WORKMEM\ WORDS+1))*100 \quad \underline{\quad} \quad \underline{\quad} \quad \underline{\quad}$$

Comparison of the Sequencing Ratio with the Working Memory Sequencing Ratio allows us an estimate of the response cost for the increased processing in working memory. Generally the proportion of sequenced responses in this index is less than in the preceding Sequencing index. This measure is reflective of the strength of the sequencing process to attentive or rehearsal processing.

The clinician must remember that these ratios are dependent upon the basic STM scores for interpretation. Thus an elevated sequencing score combined with a low working memory may suggest that the sequencing is interfering with the memory span.

A low score indicates that working memory processing functions at the expense of sequencing to a greater degree than usual.

At lower grades where the pupils are just beginning to work with written language the STM relates more the visual written form relates more heavily to reading and spelling as we see from the Ricatelli study( ) of first grade children. The sample for this study consisted of 67 primary level (first, second and third grade) children who attended a parochial school in New Haven, Connecticut. These children were of diverse ethnic background and ability level, and included students who were on, below and above grade level in reading.

Ricatelli found significant changes in the ability to read a list of vocabulary words between the October and Tne testings Correlations of the October word reading vocabulary and both visual and auditory STM with a written response were high r. = .72 for each comparison. The picture changes for the for Auditory/Oral response where the correlation is r. = .37

T

The STM measures correlated at the nearly the same level with the CTBS admininstered in June.

Short Term Memory Measures with CTBS Reading and Spelling
Grade 1, N=65

	CTBS Reading	CTBS Spelling
VSTM	.71	.71
ASTM	.35	.26
Wechsler DS	-.19	-.23

Correlations between June reading vocabulary and written response STM were visual/written (r = .71, p. < 0.01) and auditory/written (r = .67 p. < 0.01) were strong. The correlation of r. = .29 between June vocabulary and auditory/oral response was much lower although significant at the .05 level. In general, it can be concluded that STM is more involved with the more complex reading processes. It should also be noted that all reading scores changed significantly from October to June.

Ricatelli concludes,

> This study also has potential practical significance for educational intervention. Since these data did not support the auditory presentation oral response STM task as a correlate of immediate or future reading skills, support for the oral-response memory span as a screening tool with beginning readers does not seem justified. Rather it has been found that written response STM tasks do correlate well with immediate and future reading skills of first, second and third grade children. Thus, the value of STM as a predictor of reading ability for primary level students would seem to lie with the written response rather than the oral response task.

The common error that many psychologists make is to use Wechsler digit span as a measure of "memory". Aside from the fact that the reliability is limited, it tests only auditory-verbal memory for numbers. There is some MRI evidence that numbers are not processed in the same areas of the brain as words and do not use the same neural circuits. Second as Baddeley and his colleagues have pointed out, there are at least two different neural circuits for STM, an Articulatory Loop and a Visual Spatial Scratch Pad. While this as the popular position at present I think it is an over simplification, I do agree that the auditory and visual input channels differ, and there is considerable neuro-anatomical evidence to support this. To go one step further, there is also anatomical evidence that the verbal and written output channels are different and the results of a measure of memory depends upon which of these four channels are used. Further Facial memory or recognition appears to be processed using somewhat different neural channels.

References

Abas, M.A., Sahakian, B.J., Levy, R. (1990) Neuropsychological deficits and CT scan changes in elderly depressives. Psychol Med: 20(3):507-20.

Ahissar, M., Protopapas, A., Reid, M., & Merzenich, M. M., (2000). Auditory processing parallels reading abilities in adults. Proceedings of the National Academy of Sciences of the United States of America, 97(12): 6832-7.

Atkinson, R. C. & Shiffrin, R. M., (1968) Human memory: A proposed system and its control processes. In Spence, K.w., & Spence J. T., (Eds.) The psychology of learning and motivation. New York: Academic Press.

August, G. J. & Garfinkel, B. D., (1990). Comorbidity of ADHD and reading disability among clinic-referred children. Journal of Abnormal Child Psychology, 18(1) 29-45.

Avons, S. E., (1998). Serial report and item recognition of novel visual patterns. The British Journal of Psychology, 89 (Pt 2) 285-308.

Baddeley, A. D., (1986). Working Memory. Oxford, England: Clarendon Press.

Baddeley, A., (2002) Fractionating the central executive.   In D.T. Stuss & R. T. Knight (Eds.) Principles of frontal lobe function. New York: Oxford University. .

Barkley, R.A., Grodzinsky, G., & DuPaul, G.J., (1992). Frontal lobe functions in attention deficit disorder with and without hyperactivity: A review and research report. Journal of Abnormal Child Psychology, 20 163-188.

Batchelor, E. S., Gray, J. W., & Dean, R. S. (1990). Empirical testing of a cognitive model to account for neuropsychological functioning underlying arithmetic problem solving. Journal of Learning Disabilities, 23(1), 38-42.

Trevor K. Bell (1990) Rapid Sequential Processing in Dyslexic and Ordinary Readers. Perceptual and Motor Skills: Volume 71, Issue , pp. 1155-1159.

Bloomer, R.H., 1956. Word length and complexity variables in spelling difficulty. Journal of Educational Research, 49, 531-535.

Bloomer, R.H., 1959. Stimulus properties of words: Variables related to spelling difficulty. Doctoral Dissertation, University of Southern California, Microfilms #59-3509.

Bloomer, R. H., (1978) The Bloomer Learning Test. Scotland, CT: Brador Publications.

Bloomer, R. H., (1990) Working Memory of Children: Standard Scores for Letters and Words for Tasks II, III and IV of the Bloomer Learning Test. (DPSU Technical Report 90-3) Special Education Center, The University of Connecticut.

Blumstein, S.E., Byma, G., Kurowski, K., Hourihan, J., Brown, T. & Hutchinson, A., 1998, On-Line Processing of Filler–Gap Constructions in Aphasia Brain and Language Volume 61, Issue 2(1), 149–168.

Boulenger, J.-P., Fournier, M., Rosales, D., Lavallée, Y.-J., 1997. Mixed anxiety and depression: from theory to practice. J. Clin. Psychiatry 58 (suppl. 8), 27–34.

Bowey, J. A., Cain, M. T., & Ryan, S. M. (1992). A reading-level design study of phonological skills underlying fourth-grade children's word reading difficulties. Child Development, 63, 999-1011.

Buckalew,L. W. & Hickey,R. S.,(1984). Subject and Stimulus Variables in Short Term Recall and Span pd Apprehension Bulletin of the Psychonomic Society 22 (1):37-39

Campbell, R. & Butterworth. B.L. (1985). Phonological dyslexia and dysgraphia in a highly literate subject: A developmcntal case with associated deficits of phonemic processing and awareness Quarterly Journal of Experimental Psychology. 37A. 435-475

Caplan, M.Z., Weissberg, R.P., Grober, J.S,, Sivo P.J., Grady, K, Jacoby, C.,(1992). Social competence promotion with inner-city and suburban young adolescents: Effects on social adjustment and alcohol use. J Consult Clin Psychol. 1992;60:56–63.

Channon, S., Baker, J.E., Robertson, M.M., (1993).Working memory in clinical depression: an experimental study. Psychol Med. 1993 Feb;23(1):87-91.

Coltheart, M. (1989). Implicit memory and the functional architecture of cognition. In S. Lewandowsky, J.C. Dunn, & K. Kirsner (Eds.), Implicit memory: Theoretical issues. Hillsdale NJ: Lawrence Erlbaum Associates Publishers.

Comprehensive Test of Basic Skills. (1990), New York, McGraw-HILL

Cornette, L., Dupont, P., Bormans, G., Mortelmans, L., & Orban, G. A., (2001). Separate neural correlates for the mnemonic components of successive discrimination and working memory tasks Cerebral Cortex. 2001 Jan; 11(1) 59-72.

Cousens, P., Ungrer, J.J., Crawford J. A., & Stevens, M. M.M, (1991). Cognitive efects of Childhood Leukemia Therapy: A Case for Four Specific Deficits. Journal of Pediatric Psychology. 16, 475-488.

Dannenbaum, S.E., Parkinson, S. R., & Inman, v. w., (1988). Short Term Forgeting: Comparisons between Patients with Dementia of the Alzheimer Type, depressed and normal elderly. Cognitive Neuropsychology., 5, 213-233.

Delbecq-Derouesné, J., Beauvois, M.F., (1989). Memory processes and aging: A defect of automatic rather than controlled processes? Archives of Gerontology and Geriatrics, Vol Suppl 1, 121-150.

Donders, F.C., (1868, 1969) Over de snelheid van psychische processen. In W. G. Koster (Ed.) Attention and performance II, Acta Psychologia, 30 412-431.

Douglas, V.I., Benezra, E. ((1990) Supraspan verbal memory in attention deficit disorder with hyperactivity normal and reading-disabled boys. Journal of Abnormal Child Psychology. 1990;18:617–638.

Ebbinghaus, H. E. (1915) Memory: A contribution to experimental psychology (trans. H. A. Ruger & C. E. Bussenius) New York: Teacher's College, Columbia University. (Original work published 1885).

Evans, B. J. W., Drasdo, N., & Richards, I. L., (1994). Visual acuity and refractive visual factors in dyslexia. Vision Research, 34(14) 1913-1926..

Eysenck, M. W., (1979) Anxiety, learning, and memory: A reconceptualization. Journal of Research in Personality; 13(4) 363-385.

Eysenck, M. W.; & Calvo, M. G. (1992) Anxiety and performance: The processing efficiency theory. Cognition and Emotion; 6(6) 409-434

Fiez, J. A., Raife, E. A., Balota, B. A., Schwarz, J. P., Raichle, M. E., & Petersen, S. E., (1996). A positron emission tomography study of the short-term maintenance of verbal information. Journal of neuroscience, 16(2) 808-22.

Goldman-Rakic, P.S.. 1996, Regional and cellular fractionation of working memory. Proc National Academy of Science. *93* 13473-13480

Goldstein, G., Malec, E. A., (1989). Memory training for severely amnesic patients. Neuropsychology; 1989 Jan Vol 3(1) 9-16.

Greene, R. L., (1990). Spacing effects on implicit memory tests. Journal of Experimental Psychology Learning, Memory, and Cognition, 16(6) 1004-1011.

Grigsby, J., Kaye, K. & Busenbark, D., (1994). Alphanumeric sequencing: A report on a brief measure of information processing used among persons with multiple sclerosis. Perceptual and Motor Skills, 78(3, Pt 1) 883-887.

Gupta, P. C., & Dash, A. S., (1989). Effectiveness of varying instructions on recall in verbal learning. Psycho Lingua, 19(2) 71-77.

Gutbrod, K., Cohen, R., Mager, B., & Meier, E., (1989). Coding and recall of categorized material in aphasics. Journal of Clinical and Experimental Neuropsychology, 11(6) 821-841.

Hartman, M., Knopman, D. S., & Nissen, M. J., (1989). Implicit learning of new verbal associations. Journal of Experimental Psychology Learning, Memory, and Cognition, 15(6) 1070-1082.

Henry, L. A., (1991).The effects of word length and phonemic similarity in young children's short-term memory. Quarterly Journal of Experimental Psychology Human Experimental Psychology, 43A(1) 35-52.

Henry, L. A. & Millar, S.,(1993). Why does memory span improve with age? A review of the evidence for two current hypotheses. European Journal of Cognitive Psychology, 5(3) 241-287.

Henson, R. N., 1998). Short-term memory for serial order: the Start-End Model. Cognitive psychology, 36(2) 73-137.

Henson, R. N., (1999). Positional information in short-term memory: relative or absolute Memory and cognition, 27(5) 915-27.

Henson, R. N., Burgess, N., & Frith, C. D., (2000). Recoding, storage, rehearsal and grouping in verbal short-term memory: an fMRI study. Neuropsychologia, 38(4) 426-40.

James, W., (1890) The principles of Psychology. (2 vols.) New York: Henry Holt & Company.

Jonides, J., Schumacher, E. H., Smith, E. E., Koeppe, R. A., Awh, E., Reuter-Lorenz, P. A., Marshuetz, C., & Willis, C. R., (1998). The role of parietal cortex in verbal working memory. Journal of neuroscience, 18(13): 5026-34.

Kandell, E. R., Schwartz, J.H., & Jessell, T.M (2003). Principles of Neural Science, 3rd Edition. Norwalk CT: Appleton Lange

Korkman, M., & Pesonen, A. E., (1994). A comparison of neuropsychological test profiles of children with attention deficit-hyperactivity disorder and/or learning disorder. Journal of Learning Disabilities, 27(6) 383-392.

Kupietz, S. S., (1990). Sustained attention in normal and in reading-disabled youngsters with and without ADDH. Journal of Abnormal Child Psychology, 18(4) 357-372.

Lawlor, B. A., (1990). Serotonin and Alzheimer's disease. Psychiatric Annals, 20(10) 567-570.

LeDoux, J. (2003) The Emotional Brain, Fear, and the Amygdala Cellular and Molecular Neurobiology, Vol. 23, Nos. 4/5,

Levy, F., & Hobbes, G., (1989). Reading, spelling, and vigilance in attention deficit and conduct disorder. Journal of

Abnormal Child Psychology, 17(3) 291-298.

Loge, D. V., Staton, R. D., & Beatty, W. W., (1990). Performance of children with ADHD on tests sensitive to frontal lobe dysfunction.Journal of the American Academy of Child and Adolescent Psychiatry, 29(4) 540-545.

Lovett, S. B., & Flavell, J. H., (1991). Understanding and remembering: Children's knowledge about the differential effects of strategy and task variables on comprehension and memorization. Child Development, 61(6) 1842-1858.

Lumsden, E. A., (1993). Borderline personality disorder: A consequence of experiencing affect within a truncated time frame? Journal of Personality Disorders, 7(3) 265-274.

Luria, A.R. (1980). Higher cortical functions in man. New York: Basic Books.

Lyon, D. O. (1917) Memory and the learning process London: Kissinger

MacLeod, C., & Donnellan, A. M., (1993) Individual differences in anxiety and the restriction of working memory capacity. Personality and Individual Differences; 15(2) 163-173.

Markham, R.; & Darke, S., (1991) The effects of anxiety on verbal and spatial task performance. Australian Journal of Psychology; 43(2) 107-111

Miller, G. A. (1956). "The magical number seven, plus or minus two: Some limits on our capacity for processing information". Psychological Review 63 (2): 81–97.

Oberklaid, F., Harris, C., & Keir, E., (1989). Auditory dysfunction: In children with school problems. Clinical Pediatrics, 28(9) 397-403

Oberly, H.S., (1928). A comparison of the spans of *attention* and memory. Amer. J. Psychol. 40; 295-302.

Osborn, R. G., & Meador, D. M., (1990). The memory
performance of selected depressed and nondepressed
nine- to eleven-year-old male children. Behavioral
Disorders, 16(1) 32-38.

Paulesu E., Frith C.D., & Frackowiak, R.S., (1993)The neural
correlates of the verbal component of working memory.
Nature. 25;362(6418):342-5.

Parmentier, F. B., & Jones, D. M., (2000). Functional
characteristics of auditory temporal-spatial short-term
memory: evidence from serial order errors   Journal of
experimental psychology. Learning, memory, and
cognition, 26(1): 222-38.

Peynircioglu, Z. F., (1995). Covert rehearsal of tones. Journal of
Experimental Psychology Learning, Memory, and
Cognition, 21(1) 185-192.

Pickering, S. J., Gathercole, S. E., & Peaker, S. M., (1998).
Verbal and visuospatial short-term memory in children:
evidence for common and distinct mechanisms. Memory
and cognition, 26(6) 1117-30.

Plenkovic, V., (1988). Pamcenje auditivnog i vizualnog slijeda kod
autista. / Auditory and visual sequential memory of
autistic subjects. Revija za Psihologiju, 18(1-2) 43-51.

Pliszka, S. R., (1990). Effect of anxiety on cognition, behavior,
and stimulant response in ADHD. Journal of the American
Academy of Child and Adolescent Psychiatry, 28(6)
882-887.

Posner, M. I., Petersen, S. E., Fox, P. T., Raichle, M. E. (1988).
Localization of cognitive operations in the human brain.
Science, 240 1627-1631.

Rapala, M. & Brady, S. (1990). Reading ability and short-term
memory memory: The role of phonological processing.

Reading and Writing. 2: 1-25.

Rapee, R. M., (1993) The utilisation of working memory by worry. Behaviour Research and Therapy; 31(6) 617-620.

Revelle, W., (1987). Personality and motivation: Sources of inefficiency in cognitive performance. Journal of Research in Personality, 21(4) 436-452.

Ribot T. Les Maladies de la Memoire [English translation: Diseases of Memory] New York: Appleton-Century-Crofts; 1881.:

Ricitelli, J. R., (1993). Relationships between modes of short term memory (STM) tasks and besic reading processes. Doctoral Dissertations, Storrs, CT. The University of Connecticut.

Roland, P. E., Skinhöj, E., Larsen, B., & Endo, H., (1977) Perception and voluntary action: Localization of basic input and output functions, as revealed by regional cerebral blood flow increases in the human brain. In J. S. Meyer, H. Lechner, and M. Reivich (eds). Cereberal Vascular Disease. Amsterdam: Excerpta Medica.

Romine, C.B., Reynolds, C.R. (2005) A model of the development of frontal lobe functioning: findings from a meta-analysis. Appl Neuropsychol. 2005;12(4):190-201.

Romani, C., Ward, J., & Olson, A., (1999). Developmental surface dysgraphia: what is the underlying cognitive impairment? The Quarterly journal of experimental psychology, A, Human experimental psychology 52(1) 97-128.

Ronnberg, J., Larsson, C., Fogelsjoo, A., Nilsson, L. G., Lindberg, M., & Angquist, K. A., (1996). Memory dysfunction in mild aphasics. Scandinavian-journal-of-psychology, 37(1) 46-61.

Routh, D. K., (1987). Cognitive rehabilitation for children with head injury, learning disability, and mental retardation. Cognitive Rehabilitation, 5(6) 16-21.

Salthouse, T.A. (1991b). Mediation of adult age differences in cognition by reductions in working memory and speed of processing. Psychological Science, 2 , 179 - 183

Salthouse, T.A. (2009). When does age-related cognitive decline begin? Neurobiology of Aging, 30, 507-514.

Salthouse, T.A., Schroeder, D.H., Ferrer, E., 2004. Estimating retest effects in longitudinal assessments of cognitive functioning in adults between 18 and 60 years of age. Developmental Psychology 40,813–822.

Samuels, S. J., (1988) Decoding and automaticity: Helping poor readers become automatic at word recognition. Reading Teacher. 41(8) 756-760.

Santiago, H. C. & Matos, I., (1994). Visual recognition memory in specific learning-disabled children. Journal of the American Optometric Association, 65(10) 690-700.

Siegel, L. S., & Ryan, E. B., (1989). Subtypes of developmental dyslexia: The influence of definitional variables. Reading and Writing, 1(3) 257-287.

Singleton, C. H., (1988). The early diagnosis of developmental dyslexia. Support for Learning, 3(2) 108-121

Speidel G. E. 1989. Imitation: A bootstrap for learning to speak? In G. E.Speidel & K. E.Nelson (Eds.), The many faces of imitation in language learning (pp. 151- 179). New York: Springer-Verlag.

Speidel G. E. 1993. Phonological short-term memory and individual differences in learning to speak: A bilingual case study. First Language, 13, 69- 91.

Sullivan, E. T., Corkin, W. N., & Growden, J. H., (1986). Verbal and non-verbal short term memory in patients with

Alzhiemer's disease and in healthy elderly subjects, Developmental Neuropsychology, 2 387-400.

Tallon-Baudry, C., Bertrand, O., & Fischer, C., (2001).Oscillatory synchrony between human extrastriate areas during visual short-term memory maintenance. Journal of neuroscience, 21(20) RC177.

Tirosh, E., & Cohen, A., (1998). Language deficit with attention-deficit disorder: a prevalent comorbidity. Journal of child neurology, 13(10) 493-7.

Turner, L. A., Dofny, E. M. & Dutka, S., (1994). Effect of strategy and attribution training on strategy maintenance and transfer. American Journal on Mental Retardation, 98(4) 445-454.

Vernon, P. A., (1987.) Speed of Information Ptocessing and Intelligence. Norwood NJ, Ablex.

Vygotsky, L. (1934/1986). Thought and language. Cambridge, MA: MIT Press.

Waldron, K. A., & Saphire, D. G. (1990). An analysis of WISC-R factors for gifted students with learning disabilities. Journal of Learning Disabilities, 23, 491-498.

Wallace, G., & Corballis, M. C., (1973). Short-term memory and coding strategies in the deaf. Journal of Experimental Psychology, 99(3) 334-348.

Wang, A. Y. (1990). The memory-metamemory connection: Further evidence. Human Learning and Behavior, 7, 7-13.

Wang, A. Y., Thomas, M. H., Inzana, C. M., & Primicerio, L. J., (1993). Long-term retention under conditions of intentional learning and the keyword mnemonic. Bulletin of the Psychonomic Society

Weingartner, H., Eckardt, M. Grafman, J., Wolchan, S., et-al., (1993). The effects of repetition on memory performance in cognitively impaired patients. Neuropsychology, 7(3) 385-395.

Weiskrantz, L. & Warrington, E.K. (1970). A study of forgetting in amnesic patients. Neuropsychologia, 8, 281-288.

West, R. L. & Crook, T. H., (1991). Age differences in everyday memory: Laboratory analogues of telephone number recall. Psychology and Aging, 5(4) 520-529.

Whall, A. L., (1986). Identifying the characteristics of pseudodementia. Journal of Gerontological Nursing, 12(10) 34-35.

Wiegersma, S. & Meertse, K., (1990). Subjective ordering, working memory, and aging. Experimental Aging Research, 16(1-2) 73-77.

Wilding, J. M., (1984). Extroversion and memory for information in prose. Human Learning Journal of Practical Research and Applications, 3(2) 109-117.

Williams, J. K., Richman, L., & Yarbrough, D., (1991). A comparison of memory and attention in Turner syndrome and learning disability. Journal of Pediatric Psychology, 16(5) 585-593.

Wildgruber, D., Kischka, U., Ackermann, H., Klose, U., & Grodd, W., (1999). Dynamic pattern of brain activation during sequencing of word strings evaluated by fMRI. Brain research. Cognitive brain research, 7(3) 285-94.

Wold, A. H. & Reinvang, I., (1990). The relation between integration, sequence of information, short-term memory, and Token Test performance of aphasic subjects. Journal of Communication Disorders, 23(1) 31-59.

Wood, K. M., Richman, L.C., Eliason, M. J., (1989)..Immediate memory functions in reading disability subtypes; Brain Lang.;36(2):181-92.

Wood, E., Willoughby, T., Bolger, A., Younger, J., et-al., (1993). Effectiveness of elaboration strategies for grade school children as a function of academic achievement. Journal of Experimental Child Psychology, 56(2) 240-253.

Woodworth, R. S., (1938). Experimental Psychology. New York: Henry Holt & Company.

Wright, A. A., Cook, R. G., Rivera, J. J., Shyan, M. R., et-al., (1990). Naming, rehearsal, and interstimulus interval effects in memory processing. Journal of Experimental Psychology Learning, Memory, and Cognition, 16(6) 1043-1059.

Zubieta, J. K., & Alessi, N. E., (1993). Is there a role of serotonin in the disruptive behavior disorders? A literature review. Journal of Child and Adolescent Psychopharmacology, 3(1) 11-35.

Appendix A

Volume 2 STM Variables

KR-21 Reliability , Standard Error of Measurement , and Minimum Significant Difference by Grade Level

Table A-2.1. Volume 2.1 Processing in Short Term Memory
KR-21 - Reliabilities

	GRADE 1	GRADE 2	GRADE 3	GRADE 4	GRADE 5	GRADE 6	GRD 7-8	GR 9-10	ADULT	MEDIAN
VSTM	.79	.85	.86	.84	.85	.81	.81	.81	.81	.81
ASTM	.84	.84	.76	.82	.75	.81	.88	.82	.82	.82
VAPP	.88	.88	.81	.88	.77	.80	.84	.81	.81	.81
STM	.93	.92	.91	.91	.89	.80	.91	.91	.92	.91
WORK MEM-L	.80	.80	.83	.91	.80	.77	.86	.82	.86	.82
WORK MEM-W	.81	.82	.78	.78	.77	.93	.80	.77	.82	.80
STIM RATIO	.95	.95	.91	.91	.86	.86	.77	.86	.77	.86
IMPULS	.96	.96	.96	.96	.96	.96	.96	.85	.83	.96

Table A-2.2-R Volume 2.2 Processing in Short Term Memory
KR-21 - Reliabilities

	GRADE 1	GRADE 2	GRADE 3	GRADE 4	GRADE 5	GRADE 6	GRD 7-8	GR 9-10	ADULT	MEDIAN
REHERS	.99	.98	.90	.90	.90	.90	.90	.83	.83	.90
CROSS MODAL	.98	.98	.85	.85	.85	.85	.85	.85	.85	.85
STIMU MODE	.97	.94	.86	.86	.86	.86	.86	.81	.81	.86
RESP MODE	.98	.94	.94	.94	.94	.94	.94	.94	.94	.94
STIM-SEQ	.96	.90	.89	.89	.89	.89	.89	.88	.88	.89
STIM NUMBR	.95	.98	.93	.93	.93	.96	.96	.93	.92	.92

Table A-2.1.-Standard Error Volume 2.1 Processing in Short Term Memory
STANDARD ERROR OF STANDARD SCORES

	GRADE 1	GRADE 2	GRADE 3	GRADE 4	GRADE 5	GRADE 6	GRD 7-8	GR 9-10	ADULT	MEDIAN
VSTM	1.37	1.16	1.12	1.20	1.16	1.31	1.31	1.31	1.31	1.31
ASTM	1.20	1.20	1.44	1.27	1.50	1.31	1.04	1.27	1.27	1.27
VAPP	1.00	1.00	1.31	1.00	1.44	1.34	1.20	1.31	1.31	1.31
STM	.80	.85	.90	.90	1.94	.95	.90	.90	.85	.95
WORK MEM-L	1.34	1.34	1.23	.90	1.34	1.44	1.12	1.27	1.12	1.27
WORK MEM-W	1.31	1.27	1.41	1.41	1.44	.80	1.34	1.44	1.27	1.34
STIM RATIO	.67	.67	.95	.90	1.12	1.12	1.44	1.12	1.44	1.12
IMPULS	.30	.99	.60	.60	.60	.60	.60	1.16	1.23	.60

Table A-2.2- Standard Error Volume 2.2 Processing in Short Term Memory
STANDARD ERROR OF <u>STANDARD SCORES</u>

	GRADE 1	GRADE 2	GRADE 3	GRADE 4	GRADE 5	GRADE 6	GRD 7-8	GR 9-10	ADULT	MEDIAN
REHERS	.30	.42	.95	.95	.95	.95	.95	1.23	1.23	.95
CROSS MODAL	.42	.42	1.16	1.16	1.16	1.16	1.16	1.16	1.15	1.16
STIMU MODE	.52	.74	1.12	1.12	1.12	1.12	1.12	1.31	1.31	1.12
RESP MODE	.42	.74	.74	.74	.74	.74	.74	.74	.74	.74
STIM SEQUEN	.60	.95	1.00	1.00	1.00	1.00	1.00	1.04	1.04	1.00
STIM NUMBR	.67	.42	.80	.80	.80	.60	.60	.80	.80	.80
SEQ BY NUMBR	.60	.42	.74	.74	.74	.67	.67	.60	.60	.67

Table A-2.1-M.S.D.

Volume 2.1 Processing in Short Term Memory

MINIMUM SIGNIFICANT DIFFERENCE - .05 LEVEL FOR STANDARD SCORES

	GRADE 1	GRADE 2	GRADE 3	GRADE 4	GRADE 5	GRADE 6	GRD 7-8	GR 9-10	ADULT	MEDIAN
VSTM	3	3	3	3	3	3	3	3	3	3
ASTM	3	3	3	3	3	3	2	3	3	3
VAPP	2	2	3	2	3	3	3	3	3	3
STM	2	2	2	2	2	3	2	2	2	2
WORK MEM-L	3	3	3	2	3	3	3	3	3	3
WORK MEM-W	3	3	3	3	3	2	3	3	3	3
STIM RATIO	1	1	2	2	3	3	3	3	3	3
IMPULS	1	1	1	1	1	1	1	3	2	1

Table A-2.2-M.S.D. Volume 2.2 Processing in Short Term Memory

MINIMUM SIGNIFICANT DIFFERENCE - .05 LEVEL FOR STANDARD SCORES

	GRADE 1	GRADE 2	GRADE 3	GRADE 4	GRADE 5	GRADE 6	GRD 7-8	GR 9-10	ADULT	MEDIAN
REHERS	1	1	2	2	2	2	2	3	3	2
CROSS MODAL	1	1	3	3	3	3	3	3	3	3
STIMUL MODE	1	2	3	3	3	3	3	3	3	3
RESPON MODE	1	2	2	2	2	2	2	2	2	2
STIMUL SEQUEN	1	2	2	2	2	2	2	2	2	2
STIMU NUMB	1	1	2	2	2	1	1	2	2	2
SEQ BY NUMB	1	1	2	2	2	1	1	1	1	1

Appendix B

Volume II

SHORT TERM MEMORY
Variables

Tables for conversion of

RAW SCORES
INTO
STANDARD SCORES

Grade1 Table 2.1 Volume 2 Conversion of Raw Scores to Scaled Scores

Scaled Score	VSTM	ASTM	VAPP	STM	WRK-MEM LETTERS	WORKMEM WORDS	STMCOMP RATIO	IMPULSE	Scaled Score
1	1	0		1-2	0-		0-1	0-	1
2	2	1		3-5	1		2	1	2
3	3	2		6-8	2-3		3	2-3	3
4	4-5	3	0	9-17	5-7		4	4-5	4
5	6-7	4-6	1-4	18-22	8-10			6-7	5
6	8	7	5-6	23-24	11-13	-0-	5-6	8-9	6
7	9-10	8-9	7	25-30	14	1	7-13	10-12	7
8	11	10-11	8-9	31-33	15	2	14-20	13-22	8
9	12-13	12	10-11	34-38	16-18	3	21-25	23-29	9
10	14-16	13-14	12	39-45	19	4	26-30	30-37	10
11	17	15-17	13-14	46-50	20-22	5-6	31-35	38-75	11
12	18-19	18-19	15-16	51-55	23	7	36-41	76-116	12
13	20-23	20-22	17-20	56-63	24-25	8	42-51	117-124	13
14	24-25	23	21	63-70	26-29	9-12	52-54	125-138	14
15	26-28	24-26	22	71-76	30-31	13-15	55-69	139-163	15
16	29-30	27-29	23	77-83	32-33	16-19	70-86	164-171	16
17	31-32	31	24-26	84-87	34-36	20-23	87-94	172-185	17
18	33-35	32	27-28	87-95	37+	24+	95-99	186+	18
19	36+	34+	29+	96+			100		19
N'	326	312	317	311	161	161	161	59	N'
r_{tt}	.79	.84	.88	.93	.80	.81	.95	.99	r_{tt}
C_{90}	.69	.79	.91	1.19	.71	.72	1.56	3.16	C_{90}
S.E.M.	3.03	2.96	2.39	4.41	2.76	1.71	4.14	4.55	S.E.M.
M.S.D.	6	6	5	9	6	4	9	9	M.S.D.
MEAN	16.17	14.62	12.85	44.00	17.58	4.37	29.75	44.61	MEAN
S.D.	6.58	6.14	6.09	16.65	6.17	3.94	18.86	45.78	S.D.

Grade 1 - Table 2.1   Volume 2   Conversion of Raw Scores to Scaled Scores

Scaled Scores	REHEARS	CROSS MODAL	STIMULU MODE	RESPONSE MODE	STM-MEM SEQUENCE	WRK-MEM SEQUENCE	STIMULUS NUMBER	SEQUENCE BY NUMBR	Scaled Scores
1	>20	0-15	0-4	0-7	0-10	0	0-9	0-2	1
2	20-42	16-36	5-11	8-19	11-25	1-2	10-21	3-4	2
3	43-53	37-42	12-25	20-49	26-30	3-6	22-56	5-11	3
4	54-64	43-55	26-34	50-64	31-33	7-12	57-63	12-18	4
5	65-77	56-68	35-44	65-68	34-38	13-15	64-73	19-23	5
6	78-86	69-79	45-57	69-71	39-42	16-20	74-76	24-29	6
7	87-96	80-91	58-69	72-80	43-52	21-25	77-86	30-32	7
8	97-105	92-98	70-87	81-92	53-56	26-30	87-89	33-41	8
9	106-112	99-107	88-95	93-98	57-60	31-35	90-94	42-47	9
10	113-123	108-115	96-98	99-107	61-67	36-40	95-98	48-57	10
11	124-131	116-126	99-110	108-125	68-72	41-46	99-108	58-62	11
12	132-152	127-142	111-126	126-160	73-76	47-52	109-115	63-71	12
13	153-173	143-159	127-140	161-186	77-88	53-61	116-133	72-89	13
14	174-200	160-185	141-157	187-210	89-92	62-69	134-142	90-99	14
15	201-267	186-240	158-179	211-236	93-95	70-76	143-161	100-115	15
16	268-467	241-400	180-198	237-260	96-97	77-85	162-180	116-152	16
17	468+	401-525	199-280	261+	98-99	86-92	181-187	153-180	17
18	1001+	526-600	280+		100	93-95	188-220	181-300	18
19	1451+	601+				96+	221+	301+	19
'N'	308	308	180	52	191	197	191	197	'N'
r_tt	.99	.98	.97	.98	.96	.94	.95	.96	r_tt
C_90	3.16	2.25	1.83	2.25	1.56	1.32	1.43	1.56	C_90
S.E.M.	10.81	9.44	7.40	6.42	3.70	4.23	5.85	6.53	S.E.M.
M.S.D.	22	19	15	13	8	9	12	13	M.S.D.
MEAN	143.02	127.17	98.69	111.64	65.16	40.73	103.82	47.46	MEAN
S.D.	128.48	73.38	39.32	48.61	16.77	18.04	27.34	32.67	S.D.

Grade 2 Table 2.2 Volume 2 Conversion of Raw Scores to Scaled Scores

Scaled Score	VSTM	ASTM	VAPP	STM	WRK-MEM LETTERS	WRK-MEM WORDS	STIMCOMP RATIO	IMPULSE	Scaled Score
1	0-1			1-2	-0-		0-1	0-1	1
2	2	0		3-8	1-4		2-3	2	2
3	3	1	0	9-12	5-8		4	3	3
4	4-5	2-3	1	13-22	9-11		5-7	4-5	4
5	6-8	4-7	2-4	23-28	12	-0-	8-11	6-8	5
6	9-10	8-9	5-8	29-32	13-14	1	12-15	9-10	6
7	11-13	10-11	9-10	33-38	15-16	2	16-22	11-13	7
8	14-16	12-14	11-13	39-45	17-19	3-4	23-28	14-18	8
9	17-18	15-16	14-15	46-49	20-22	5-6	29-40	19-22	9
10	19-20	17-19	16-17	50-55	23	7	41-48	23-27	10
11	21-23	20-21	18-20	56-61	24-26	8-9	49-54	28-34	11
12	24-26	22-24	21-22	62-67	27-29	10-11	55-64	35-41	12
13	27-29	25-26	23	68-74	30	12-14	65-72	42-60	13
14	30-31	27	24-26	75-79	31-32	15	73-79	61-64	14
15	32-33	28-30	27-30	80-82	33-39	16-17	80-84	65-93	15
16	34-39	31-32	31-33	83-89	40-41	18-19	85-88	94-145	16
17	40-42	33-35	34-35	90-100	42-47	20-23	89-93	146-318	17
18	43-45	36-38	36+	101-115	48	24-27	94-121	319-400	18
19	46+	39+		116+		28+	122+	401+	19
N'	338	326	317	324	246	246	246	148	N'
r_tt	.85	.84	.88	.92	.80	.82	.95	.99	r_tt
C_90	.82	.79	.91	1.12	.71	.75	1.56	3.16	C_90
S.E.M.	3.08	2.80	2.65	5.02	3.28	2.20	5.63	5.25	S.E.M.
M.S.D.	7	6	6	10	7	5	11	10	M.S.D.
MEAN	16.17	18.77	14.56	53.62	21.27	8.10	45.16	36.36	MEAN
S.D.	6.58	6.99	7.04	17.65	7.34	5.22	25.24	47.01	S.D

Grade 2 - Table 2.2. Volume 2.2 Conversion of Raw Scores to Scaled Scores

Scaled Scores	REHEARSE	CROSS MODAL	STIMULUS MODE	RESPONSE MODE	STM-MEM SEQUENCE	WORK-MEM SEQUENCE	STIMULUS NUMBER	SEQUENCE BY NUMBR	Scaled Scores
1	0-9	0-8	0-10	0-6	0-7	0-2	0-13	0-	1
2	10-24	9-18	11-23	7-16	8-20	3-6	14-36	1-3	2
3	25-56	19-40	24-51	17-36	21-36	7-15	37-49	4-9	3
4	57-64	41-58	52-56	37-42	37-39	15-17	50-56	10-19	4
5	65-81	59-71	57-61	43-46	40-46	18-22	57-62	20-25	5
6	82-85	72-79	62-63	47-48	47-49	23-25	63-70	26-31	6
7	86-95	80-90	64-68	49-54	50-57	26-30	71-77	32-36	7
8	96-105	91-98	69-76	55-63	58-60	31-34	78-85	37-44	8
9	106-117	99-107	77-80	64-68	61-66	35-41	86-91	45-57	9
10	118-128	108-119	81-87	69-74	67-72	42-46	92-98	58-65	10
11	129-136	120-129	88-90	75-80	73-76	47-56	99-103	66-72	11
12	137-154	130-145	91-97	81-86	77-79	57-63	104-114	73-83	12
13	155-177	146-176	98-109	87-95	80-88	64-71	115-127	84-115	13
14	178-193	177-208	110-115	96-113	89-90	72-74	128-135	116-138	14
15	194-225	209-266	116-120	114-133	91-95	75-87	136-161	139-167	15
16	226-287	267-325	121-138	134-139	96-97	88-90	162-242	168-199	16
17	288-500	326-400	139-145	140-157	98	91-97	243-466	200-242	17
18	501-866	401-475	146-177	158-214	99	98-99	467-600	243-250	18
19	877+	476+	178+	215+	100	100+	601+	251+	19
'N'	325	325	149	149	157	168	325	168	'N'
r_{tt}	.98	.98	.94	.94	.90	.95	.98	.98	r_{tt}
C_{90}	2.25	2.25	1.32	1.32	1.00	1.43	2.25	2.25	C_{90}
S.E.M.	10.36	9.16	4.93	6.34	4.74	4.62	8.98	6.37	S.E.M.
M.S.D.	21	18	10	13	10	9	18	13	M.S.D.
MEAN	134.67	127.14	86.08	75.40	69.36	47.75	104.64	69.51	MEAN
S.D.	70.74	60.14	19.94	25.13	15.07	19.63	62.17	41.61	S.D.

Grade 3 Table 2.3 Volume 2 Conversion of Raw Scores to Scaled Scores

Scaled Score	VSTM	ASTM	VAPP	STM	WRK-MEM LETTERS	WRK-MEM WORDS	STIMCOMP RATIO	IMPULSE	Scaled Score
1	0-4	0-1	0-2	0-10	-0-	-0-	0-2	-0-	1
2	5-6	2-3	3-4	11-21	1-2	1	3-7	1-2	2
3	7-11	4-6	5-7	22-29	3-6	2	8-19	3	3
4	12-13	7-12	8-10	30-41	7-10	3	20-25	4-5	4
5	14-15	13-15	11-13	42-47	11-12	4	26-32	6-7	5
6	16-18	16-17	14-16	48-56	13-17	5	33-42	8-9	6
7	19-22	18-19	16	57-61	18-19	6-7	43-49	10-12	7
8	23-24	20-21	17-20	62-66	20-21	8-9	50-54	13-14	8
9	25-26	22-23	21	67-72	22-23	10	55-60	15-17	9
10	27-28	24	22-23	73-77	24-26	11-13	61-66	18-21	10
11	29	25-27	24-25	78-81	27	14-15	67-69	22-27	11
12	30-31	27-27	26-27	82-86	28-30	16	70-74	28-33	12
13	32-33	29-30	28-30	87-90	31-32	17-19	75-80	34-42	13
14	34-35	31	31	91-93	33-34	20	81-87	43-49	14
15	36-37	32	32	94-98	35-36	21-23	88-92	50-74	15
16	38	33-34	33-35	99-102	37	24	93-103	75-102	16
17	39-40	35-36	36-38	103-109	38-42	25-26	104-105	103-115	17
18	41-42	37-38	39-40	110-117	43-47	27-32	106-112	116-200	18
19	43+	39+	41+	118+	48	33+	113+	201+	19
'N'	253	274	317	249	228	228	228	942	'N'
r_tt	.86	.76	.81	.91	.83	.78	.91	.96	r_tt
C_90	.84	.64	.72	1.05	.77	.67	1.05	1.56	C_90
S.E.M.	2.38	2.77	2.73	4.62	2.74	2.60	5.76	4.49	S.E.M.
M.S.D.	5	6	6	10	6	6	12	9	M.S.D.
MEAN	27.20	24.18	22.89	74.39	25.21	12.96	62.67	25.56	MEAN
S.D.	6.33	5.96	6.25	15.11	6.66	5.57	18.65	22.621.	S.D

Grade 3 Table 2.3 Volume 2 Conversion of Raw Scores to Scaled Scores

Scaled Scores	REHEARSE	CROSS MODAL	STIMULUS MODE *	RESPONSE MODE *	STM-MEM SEQUENCE	WRK-MEM SEQUENCE	STIMULUS NUMBER	SEQUENCE BY NUMBR	Scaled Scores
1	0-41	0-18	0-18	0-6	0-9	0-3	0-20	0-6	1
2	42-56	19-55	19-42	7-16	10-35	4-10	21-57	7-12	2
3	57-74	56-67	43-52	17-36	35-41	11-16	58-63	13-19	3
4	74-85	68-75	53-59	37-42	42-44	17-19	64-65	20-25	4
5	86-92	76-83	60-67	43-46	45-47	20-22	66-67	26-30	5
6	93-96	84-87	68-71	47-48	48-49	23-24	68-70	31-34	6
7	97-103	88-95	72-78	49-54	50-54	25-28	71-75	35-41	7
8	104-109	96-98	79-83	55-63	55-59	29-32	76-79	42-46	8
9	110-114	99-104	84-88	64-68	60-62	33-37	80-84	47-51	9
10	115-121	105-109	89-93	69-74	63-67	38-42	85-88	52-56	10
11	122-127	110-115	94-96	75-80	68-69	43-46	89-93	57-63	11
12	128-135	116-121	97-103	81-86	79-73	47-50	94-97	64-71	12
13	136-147	122-131	104-111	87-95	74-77	51-56	98-108	72-79	13
14	148-156	132-136	112-116	96-113	78-79	57-60	109-115	80-85	14
15	157-174	137-144	117-125	114-133	80-86	61-64	116-127	86-96	15
16	175-200	145-176	126-147	134-139	87-89	65-69	128-147	97-104	16
17	201-269	177-209	148-178	140-157	90-95	70-73	148-187	105-111	17
18	270-355	210-260	179-257	158-214	96-100	74-78	188-246	112-118	18
19	356+	261+	258+	215+		79+	247+	119+	19
'N'	1414	1791	1378	149	427	467	957	367	'N'
r_{tt}	.90	.85	.86	.94	.89	.92	.93	.94	r_{tt}
C_{90}	1.00	.82	.84	1.32	.96	1.12	1.19	1.32	C_{90}
S.E.M.	8.54	8.99	7.38	6.34	3.78	3.70	5.45	4.80	S.E.M.
M.S.D.	17	18	15	13	8	8	11	10	M.S.D.
MEAN	121.87	110.07	91.86	75.40	64.68	40.70	90.29	56.74	MEAN
S.D.	27.60	23.49	19.84	25.13	11.58	12.90	20.80	19.34	S.D.

Gade 4 Table 2.4 Volume 2

Conversion of Raw Scores to Scaled Scores

Scaled Score	VSTM	ASTM	VAPP	STM	WRK-MEM LETTERS	WRK-MEM WORDS	STIMCOMP RATIO	IMPULSE	Scaled Score
1	0-3	0-5	0-7	0-14	0-3	0-	0-2	0-	1
2	4-5	6-7	8-9	15-28	4-10	1	3-7	1-2	2
3	6-8	8-11	10-11	29-48	11-13	2-4	8-19	3	3
4	9-12	12-17	12-15	49-55	14-16	5	20-25	4-5	4
5	13-17	18-20	16	56-63	17-19	6-7	26-32	6-7	5
6	18-21	21-22	17-18	64-68	20-21	8-9	33-42	8-9	6
7	22-25	23-24	19-21	69-75	22-24	10-11	43-49	10-12	7
8	26-27	25	22	76-79	25	12-13	50-54	13-14	8
9	28-29	26-27	23-24	80-83	26-27	14-15	55-60	15-17	9
10	30-31	28	25-26	84-88	28-29	16	61-66	18-21	10
11	32-33	29-30	27	89-91	30-31	17-18	67-69	22-27	11
12	34-35	31	28	92-95	32-33	19-20	70-74	28-33	12
13	36-37	32-33	29-30	96-100	34-35	21	75-80	34-42	13
14	38	34	31	101-102	36	22	81-87	43-49	14
15	39	35-36	32-33	103-106	37-38	23-24	88-92	50-74	15
16	40-41	37	34-35	107-109	39	25	93-103	75-102	16
17	42-43	38-39	36-37	110-111	40-42	26	104-105	103-115	17
18	44-45	40-42	38-39	112-113	43-44	27-32	106-112	116-200	18
19	46+	43+	40+	114+	45+	33+	113+	201+	19
'N'	415	342	372	339	374	374	228	942	'N'
r_{tt}	.84	.82	.88	.91	.91	.78	.91	.96	r_{tt}
C_{90}	.79	.75	.91	1.05	1.05	.67	1.05	1.56	C_{90}
S.E.M.	2.80	2.20	1.75	4.09	1.79	2.39	5.76	4.49	S.E.M.
M.S.D.	6	5	4	8	4	5	12	9	M.S.D.
MEAN	30.14	28.26	25.49	85.21	29.17	16.25	62.67	25.56	MEAN
S.D.	7.06	5.12	5.08	13.72	5.90	5.11	18.65	22.62	S.D.

GRADE 4 Table 2.4 Volume 2 Conversion of Raw Scores to Scaled Scores

Scaled Scores	REHEARSE	CROSS MODAL	STIMULUS MODE *	RESPONSE MODE *	STM-MEM SEQUENCE	WRK-MEM SEQUENCE	STIMULUS NUMBER	SEQUENCE BY NUMBR	Scaled Scores
1	0-41	0-18	0-18	0-6	0-9	0-3	0-20	0-6	1
2	42-56	19-55	19-42	7-16	10-35	4-10	21-57	7-12	2
3	57-74	56-67	43-52	17-36	35-41	11-16	58-63	13-19	3
4	74-85	68-75	53-59	37-42	42-44	17-19	64-65	20-25	4
5	86-92	76-83	60-67	43-46	45-47	20-22	66-67	26-30	5
6	93-96	84-87	68-71	47-48	48-49	23-24	68-70	31-34	6
7	97-103	88-95	72-78	49-54	50=54	25-28	71-75	35-41	7
8	104-109	96-98	79-83	55-63	55-59	29-32	76-79	42-46	8
9	110-114	99-104	84-88	64-68	60-62	33-37	80-84	47-51	9
10	115-121	105-109	89-93	69-74	63-67	38-42	85-88	52-56	10
11	122-127	110-115	94-96	75-80	68-69	43-46	89-93	57-63	11
12	128-135	116-121	97-103	81-86	79-73	47-50	94-97	64-71	12
13	136-147	122-131	104-111	87-95	74-77	51-56	98-108	72-79	13
14	148-156	132-136	112-116	96-113	78-79	57-60	109-115	80-85	14
15	157-174	137-144	117-125	114-133	80-86	61-64	116-127	86-96	15
16	175-200	145-176	126-147	134-139	87-89	65-69	128-147	97-104	16
17	201-269	177-209	148-178	140-157	90-95	70-73	148-187	105-111	17
18	270-355	210-260	179-257	158-214	96-100	74-78	188-246	112-118	18
19	356+	261+	258+	215+		79+	247+	119+	19
'N'	1414	1791	1378	149	427	467	957	367	'N'
r_tt	.90	.85	.86	.94	.89	.92	.93	.94	r_tt
C_{90}	1.00	.82	.84	1.32	.96	1.12	1.19	1.32	C_{90}
S.E.M.	8.54	8.99	7.38	6.34	3.78	3.70	5.45	4.80	S.E.M.
M.S.D.	17	18	15	13	8	8	11	10	M.S.D.
MEAN S.D.	121.87	110.07	91.86	75.40	64.68	40.70	90.29	56.74	MEAN S.D.
	27.60	23.49	19.84	25.13	11.58	12.90	20.80	19.34	

Grade 5 Table 2.5 Volume 2 Conversion of Raw Scores to ScaledScores

Scaled Score	VSTM	ASTM	VAPP	STM	WRK-MEM LETTERS	WRK-MEM WORDS	STIMCOMP RATIO	IMPULSE	Scaled Score
1	0-7	0-4	0-5	0-15	0-3	0-1	0-9	0-	1
2	8-12	5-9	6-8	16-31	4-10	2-5	10-22	1-2	2
3	13-16	10-15	9-10	32-52	11-14	6	23-33	3	3
4	17-18	16-17	11-14	53-63	15-19	7-8	34-42	4-5	4
5	19-22	18-19	15-17	64-68	20	9-10	43-50	6-7	5
6	23-24	20-21	18-19	69-71	21-22	11-12	51-54	8-9	6
7	25-27	22-23	20-21	72-78	23-25	13-14	55-59	10-12	7
8	28-30	24-25	22-23	79-82	26-27	15-16	60-63	13-14	8
9	31-32	26-27	24-25	83-86	28-30	17-19	64-68	15-17	9
10	33-34	28	26-27	87-90	31-32	20	69-72	18-21	10
11	35-36	29-30	28-29	91-95	33	21	73-76	22-27	11
12	37-38	31	30-31	96-99	34-36	22-23	77-80	28-33	12
13	39-41	32-34	32-33	100-104	37-39	24-25	81-85	34-42	13
14	42	34	34-35	105-107	40	26-28	85-88	43-49	14
15	43-44	36-37	36-37	108-111	41-42	29-33	89-94	50-74	15
16	45	38	38-39	112-117	43-44	34-35	95-102	75-102	16
17	46	39-40	40-42	118-121	45	36-44	103-111	103-115	17
18	47-48	41-42	43-45	122-129	46-47	45+	112-136	116-200	18
19		43+	46+	129+	48		137+	201+	19
N'	277	242	241	239	730	730	1098	942	N'
r_tt	.85	.75	.77	.89	.80	.77	.86	.96	r_tt
C_90	.82	.63	.66	.96	.75	.66	.84	1.56	C_90
S.E.M.	2.57	2.60	2.86	4.63	3.11	3.19	5.29	4.49	S.E.M.
M.S.D.	6	6	6	9	6	7	11	9	M.S.D.
MEAN	32.95	28.25	26.88	89.03	31.32	18.69	70.18	25.56	MEAN
S.D.	7.02	5.22	6.02	14.19	6.88	6.66	14.36	22.62	S.D.

Grade 5 Table 2.5 Volume 2 Conversion of Raw Scores to Scaled Scores

Scaled Scores	REHEARS	CROSS MODAL	STIMULU MODE*	RESPONSE MODE*	STM-MEM SEQUENCE	WRKMEM SEQUENCE	STIMULU NUMBER	SEQUENC BY NUMBR	Scaled Scores
1	0-41	0-18	0-18	0-6	0-9	0-3	0-20	0-6	1
2	42-56	19-55	19-42	7-16	10-35	4-10	21-57	7-12	2
3	57-74	56-67	43-52	17-36	35-41	11-16	58-63	13-19	3
4	74-85	68-75	53-59	37-42	42-44	17-19	64-65	20-25	4
5	86-92	76-83	60-67	43-46	45-47	20-22	66-67	26-30	5
6	93-96	84-87	68-71	47-48	48-49	23-24	68-70	31-34	6
7	97-103	88-95	72-78	49-54	50-54	25-28	71-75	35-41	7
8	104-109	96-98	79-83	55-63	55-59	29-32	76-79	42-46	8
9	110-114	99-104	84-88	64-68	60-62	33-37	80-84	47-51	9
10	115-121	105-109	89-93	69-74	63-67	38-42	85-88	52-56	10
11	122-127	110-115	94-96	75-80	68-69	43-46	89-93	57-63	11
12	128-135	116-121	97-103	81-86	70-73	47-50	94-97	64-71	12
13	136-147	122-131	104-111	87-95	74-77	51-56	98-108	72-79	13
14	148-156	132-136	112-116	96-113	78-79	57-60	109-115	80-85	14
15	157-174	137-144	117-125	114-133	80-86	61-64	116-127	86-96	15
16	175-200	145-176	126-147	134-139	87-89	65-69	128-147	97-104	16
17	201-269	177-209	148-178	140-157	90-95	70-73	148-187	105-111	17
18	270-355	210-260	179-257	158-214	96-100	74-78	188-246	112-118	18
19	356+	261+	258+	215+		79+	247+	119+	19
N'	1414	1791	1378	149	427	467	957	367	N'
r_{tt}	.90	.85	.86	.94	.89	.92	.93	.94	r_{tt}
C_{90}	1.00	.82	.84	1.32	.96	1.12	1.19	1.32	C_{90}
S.E.M.	8.54	8.99	7.38	6.34	3.78	3.70	5.45	4.80	S.E.M.
M.S.D.	17	18	15	13	8	8	11	10	M.S.D.
MEAN	121.87	110.07	91.86	75.40	64.68	40.70	90.29	56.74	MEAN
S.D.	27.60	23.49	19.84	25.13	11.58	12.90	20.80	19.34	S.D.

Grade 6 Table 2.6 Volume 2 Conversion of Raw Scores to Scaled Scores

Scaled Score	VSTM	ASTM	VAPP	STM	WRK-MEM LETTERS	WRK-MEM WORDS	STIMCOMP RATIO	IMPULSE	Scaled Score
1	0-7	0-3	0-5	0-14	0-3	0-1	0-9	-0	1
2	8-12	4-6	6-8	15-28	4-10	2-5	10-22	1-2	2
3	13-16	7-12	9-10	29-31	11-14	6	23-33	3	3
4	17-18	13-15	11-15	32-52	15-19	7-8	34-42	4-5	4
5	19-22	16-19	16-19	53-68	20	9-10	43-50	6-7	5
6	23-24	20-21	20	69-72	21-22	11-12	51-54	8-9	6
7	25-27	22-24	21-24	73-80	23-25	13-14	55-59	10-12	7
8	28-30	25-26	25-26	81-85	26-27	15-16	60-63	13-14	8
9	31-32	27-28	27-28	86-89	28-30	17-19	64-68	15-17	9
10	33-34	29-30	29-30	90-96	31-32	20	69-72	18-21	10
11	35-36	31-33	31	97-101	33	21	73-76	22-27	11
12	37-38	34-35	32-33	102-106	34-36	22-23	77-80	28-33	12
13	39-41	36-37	34	107-113	37-39	24-25	81-85	34-42	13
14	42	38	35-36	114-116	40	26-28	85-88	43-49	14
15	43-44	39-40	37-38	117-119	41-42	29-33	89-94	50-74	15
16	45	41-42	39	120-121	43-44	34-35	95-102	75-102	16
17	46	43	40-42	122-124	45	36-44	103-111	103-115	17
18	47-48	44-45	43-47	125-128	46-47	45+	112-136	116-200	18
19		46+	48	129+	48		137+	201+	19
N'	1100	257	257	239	730	730	1098	942	N'
r_π	.81	.81	.80	.93	.80	.77	.86	.96	r_π
C_{90}	.72	.72	.71	1.19	.75	.66	.84	1.56	C_{90}
S.E.M.	2.84	2.96	2.89	4.47	3.11	3.19	5.29	4.49	S.E.M.
M.S.D.	6	6	6	9	6	7	11	9	M.S.D.
MEAN	33.24	29.83	26.88	93.08	31.32	18.69	70.18	25.56	MEAN
S.D.	3.84	6.83	6.02	17.05	6.88	6.66	14.36	22.62	S.D.

Grade 6   Table 2.6   Volume 2   Conversion of Raw Scores to Scaled Scores

Scales Scores	REHEARSE	CROSS MODAL	STIMULUS MODE *	RESPONSE MODE *	STM-MEM SEQUENCE	WRK-MEM SEQUENCE	STIMULUS NUMBER	SEQUENCE BY NUMBR	Scaled Scores
1	0-41	0-18	0-18	0-6	0-9	0-3	0-20	1-2	1
2	42-56	19-55	19-42	7-16	10-35	4-10	21-57	3-6	2
3	57-74	56-67	43-52	17-36	35-41	11-16	58-59	7-16	3
4	74-85	68-75	53-59	37-42	42-44	17-19	60-61	17-26	4
5	86-92	76-83	60-67	43-46	45-47	20-22	62-64	27-28	5
6	93-96	84-87	68-71	47-48	48-49	23-24	65-67	29-32	6
7	97-103	88-95	72-78	49-54	50-54	25-28	68-71	33-41	7
8	104-109	96-98	79-83	55-63	55-59	29-32	71-75	42-44	8
9	110-114	99-104	84-88	64-68	60-62	33-37	76-79	45-52	9
10	115-121	105-109	89-93	69-74	63-67	38-42	80-83	53-57	10
11	122-127	110-115	94-96	75-80	68-69	43-46	84-88	58-63	11
12	128-135	116-121	97-103	81-86	70-73	47-50	89-93	64-75	12
13	136-147	122-131	104-111	87-95	74-77	51-56	94-102	76-82	13
14	148-156	132-136	112-116	96-113	78-79	57-60	103-105	83-89	14
15	157-174	137-144	117-125	114-133	80-86	61-64	106-113	90-99	15
16	175-200	145-176	126-147	134-139	87-89	65-69	114-118	100-112	16
17	201-269	177-209	148-178	140-157	90-95	70-73	119-126	113-131	17
18	270-355	210-260	179-257	158-214	96-100	74-78	127-233	132-139	18
19	356+	261+	258+	215+		79+	234+	140+	19
'N'	1414	1791	1378	149	427	467	457	100	'N'
r_{tt}	.90	.85	.86	.94	.89	.92	.96	.95	r_{tt}
C_{90}	1.00	.82	.84	1.32	.96	1.12	1.56	1.43	C_{90}
S.E.M.	8.54	8.99	7.38	6.34	3.78	3.70	5.14	5.02	S.E.M.
M.S.D.	17	18	15	13	8	8	10	10	M.S.D.
MEAN	121.87	110.07	91.86	75.40	64.68	40.70	84.75	58.55	MEAN
S.D.	27.60	23.49	19.84	25.13	11.58	12.90	24.68	22.31	S.D.

GRADE 7-8   Table 2.7-8   Volume 2   Conversion of Raw Scores to Scaled Scores

Scaled Score	VSTM	ASTM	VAPP	STM	STIMCOMP RATIO	WRK-MEM LETTERS	WRK-MEM WORDS	IMPULSE	Scaled Score
1	0-7	0-4	0-2	0-14	0-9	0-3	0-1	-0-	1
2	8-12	5-9	3-4	15-28	10-22	4-10	2-5	1-2	2
3	13-16	10-14	5-6	28-38	23-33	11-14	6	3	3
4	17-18	15-17	7-12	39-40	34-42	15-19	6	4-5	4
5	19-22	18	13-16	41-57	43-50	20	7-8	6-7	5
6	23-24	19-21	17-19	58-62	51-54	21-22	9-10	8-9	6
7	25-27	22-25	20-23	63-75	55-59	23-25	11-12	10-12	7
8	28-30	26-27	24-25	76-85	60-63	26-27	13-14	13-14	8
9	31-32	28-30	26-27	86-90	64-68	28-30	15-16	15-17	9
10	33-34	31-32	28-29	91-97	69-72	31-32	17-19	18-21	10
11	35-36	33	30-31	98-101	73-76	33	20	22-27	11
12	37-38	34-35	32-34	102-106	77-80	34-36	21	28-33	12
13	39-41	36-37	35-36	107-114	81-85	37-39	22-23	34-42	13
14	42	38-39	37-38	115-119	85-88	40	24-25	43-49	14
15	43-44	40	39	120-123	89-94	41-42	26-28	50-74	15
16	45	41-42	40-41	124	95-102	43-44	29-33	75-102	16
17	46	43-44	42-45	125-126	103-111	45	34-35	103-115	17
18	47-48	45-46	46-47	127-128	112-136	46-47	36-44	116-200	18
19		47+	48	129+	137+	48	45+	201+	19
'N'	1465	116	127	113	1098	730	730	942	'N'
r_{tt}	.81	.88	.84	.95	.86	.80	.77	.96	r_{tt}
C_{90}	.72	.91	.79	1.43	.84	.75	.66	1.56	C_{90}
S.E.M.	3.07	2.46	2.91	4.71	5.29	3.11	3.19	4.49	S.E.M.
M.S.D.	6	5	5	10	11	6	7	9	M.S.D.
MEAN	33.24	30.42	28.69	91.35	70.18	31.32	18.69	25.56	MEAN
S.D.	6.84	7.00	7.34	21.43	14.36	6.88	6.66	22.62	S.D.

Grade 7-8 Table 2.7-8   Volume 2   Conversion of Raw Scores to Scaled Scores

Scaled Scores	REHEARSE	CROSS MODAL	STIMULUS MODE*	RESPONSE MODE*	STM-MEM SEQUENCE	WRK-MEM SEQUENCE	STIMULUS NUMBER	SEQUENCE BY NUMBR	Scaled Scores
	0-41	0-18	0-18	0-6	0-9	0-3	0-20	1-2	1
	42-56	19-55	19-42	7-16	10-35	4-10	21-57	3-6	2
	57-74	56-67	43-52	17-36	35-41	11-16	58-59	7-16	3
	74-85	68-75	53-59	37-42	42-44	17-19	60-61	17-26	4
	86-92	76-83	60-67	43-46	45-47	20-22	62-64	27-28	5
	93-96	84-87	68-71	47-48	48-49	23-24	65-67	29-32	6
	97-103	88-95	72-78	49-54	50-54	25-28	68-71	33-41	7
	104-109	96-98	79-83	55-63	55-59	29-32	71-75	42-44	8
	110-114	99-104	84-88	64-68	60-62	33-37	76-79	45-52	9
	115-121	105-109	89-93	69-74	63-67	38-42	80-83	53-57	10
	122-127	110-115	94-96	75-80	68-69	43-46	84-88	58-63	11
	128-135	116-121	97-103	81-86	70-73	47-50	89-93	64-75	12
	136-147	122-131	104-111	87-95	74-77	51-56	94-102	76-82	13
	148-156	132-136	112-116	96-113	78-79	57-60	103-105	83-89	14
	157-174	137-144	117-125	114-133	80-86	61-64	106-113	90-99	15
	175-200	145-176	126-147	134-139	87-89	65-69	114-118	100-112	16
	201-269	177-209	148-178	140-157	90-95	70-73	119-126	113-131	17
	270-355	210-260	179-257	158-214	96-100	74-78	127-233	132-139	18
	356+	261+	258+	215+		79+	234+	140+	19
'N'	1414	1791	1378	149	427	467	457	100	'N'
r_{tt}	.90	.85	.86	.94	.89	.92	.96	.95	r_{tt}
C_{90}	1.00	.82	.84	1.32	.96	1.12	1.56	1.43	C_{90}
S.E.M.	8.54	8.99	7.38	6.34	3.78	3.70	5.14	5.02	S.E.M.
M.S.D.	17	18	15	13	8	8	10	10	M.S.D.
MEAN	121.87	110.07	91.86	75.40	64.68	40.70	84.75	58.55	MEAN
S.D.	27.60	23.49	19.84	25.13	11.58	12.90	24.68	22.31	S.D.

Grade 9-10   Table 2.9-10   Volume 2   Conversion of Raw Scores to Scaled Scores

Scaled Score	VSTM	ASTM	VAPP	STM	WRK-MEM LETTERS	WRK-MEM WORDS	STIMCOMP RATIO	IMPULSE	Scaled Score
1	0-7	0-7	0-5	0-21	0-3	0-1	0-9	0-2	1
2	8-12	8-14	6-12	22-47	4-9	2-5	10-22	3-4	2
3	13-16	15-16	13-16	48-67	10-17	6	23-33	5	3
4	17-18	17-18	17-20	68-69	18-20	7-8	34-42	6	4
5	19-22	19-21	21-22	70-73	21-24	9-10	43-50	7	5
6	23-24	22-25	23	74-82	25-27	11-12	51-54	8-9	6
7	25-27	26-28	24-27	83-89	28-30	13-14	55-59	10-11	7
8	28-30	29-31	28-29	90-94	31-32	15-16	60-63	12	8
9	31-32	32-33	30-31	95-99	33-34	17-19	64-68	13-14	9
10	33-34	34-35	32-33	100-102	35-37	20	69-72	15-16	10
11	35-36	36	34-35	103-105	38	21	73-76	17-18	11
12	37-38	37-38	36-37	106-108	39-40	22-23	77-80	19-23	12
13	39-41	39-40	38	109-114	41	24-25	81-85	24-26	13
14	42	41	39	115-116	42	26-28	85-88	27-30	14
15	43-44	42-43	40	117-122	43	29-33	89-94	31-40	15
16	45	44	41	123-124	44	34-35	95-102	41-51	16
17	46	45	42-43	125-128	45	36-44	103-111	52-76	17
18	47-48	46-48	44-45	129-134	46-47	45+	112-136	76+	18
19			46+	135+	48		137+		19
'N'	1465	246	252	136	167	730	1098	220	'N'
r_{tt}	.81	.82	.81	.91	.82	.77	.86	.85	r_{tt}
C_{90}	.72	.75	.72	1.05	.75	.66	.84	.82	C_{90}
S.E.M.	3.07	2.55	2.36	4.30	2.71	3.19	5.29	3.38	S.E.M.
M.S.D.	6	5	5	9	6	7	11	7	M.S.D.
MEAN	33.24	33.93	31.49	99.71	35.53	18.69	70.18	15.35	MEAN
S.D.1	6.84	5.97	5.22	14.13	6.36	6.66	14.36	8.56	S.D.

Grade 9-10   Table 2.9-10   Volume 2   Conversion of Raw Scores to Scaled Scores

Scaled Scores	REHEARSE	CROSS MODAL	STIMULUS MODE*	RESPONSE MODE*	STM-MEM SEQUENCE	WRK-MEM SEQUENCE	STIMULUS NUMBER	SEQUENCE BY NUMBR	Scaled Scores
1	0-31	0-18	0-20	0-6	0-9	0-8	0-20	1-10	1
2	32-72	19-55	21-49	7-16	10-38	9-18	21-50	11-22	2
3	73-81	56-67	50-67	17-36	39-50	19-24	51-53	23-29	3
4	82-86	68-75	68-77	37-42	51-54	25-27	54-55	30-35	4
5	87-89	76-83	78-81	43-46	55-58	28-30	56-58	36-43	5
6	90-94	84-87	82-86	47-48	59-62	31-35	59-60	44-47	6
7	95-99	88-95	87-91	49-54	63-67	36-42	61-64	48-57	7
8	100-102	96-98	92-96	55-63	68-70	43-46	65-66	58-62	8
9	103-105	99-104	97-98	64-68	71-75	47-50	67-70	63-70	9
10	106-109	105-109	99-102	69-74	76-79	51-54	71-74	71-77	10
11	110-114	110-115	103-106	75-80	80-81	55-59	75-79	78-81	11
12	115-119	116-121	107-111	81-86	82-83	60-64	80-84	82-91	12
13	120-126	122-131	112-116	87-95	84-86	65-68	85-91	92-103	13
14	127-132	132-136	117-119	96-113	87-88	69-70	92-97	104-110	14
15	133-144	137-144	120-125	114-133	89-91	71-72	98-106	111-123	15
16	145-154	145-176	126-132	134-139	92-93	73-75	107-111	124-130	16
17	155-163	177-209	133-141	140-157	94-95	76-79	112-120	131-133	17
18	164-186	210-260	142-155	158-214	96-98	80-82	121-129	134-140	18
19	187+	261+	156+	215+	99-100	83+	130+	141+	19
'N'	377	1791	389	149	218	218	377	159	'N'
r_{tt}	.83	.85	.81	.94	.88	.92	.93	.96	r_{tt}
C_{90}	.79	.82	.72	1.32	.91	1.12	1.19	1.83	C_{90}
S.E.M.	6.56	8.99	5.87	6.34	3.64	3.67	3.82	4.68	S.E.M.
M.S.D.	13	18	12	13	8	8	8	9	M.S.D.
MEAN	110.35	110.07	101.53	75.40	74.69	52.78	75.36	75.60	MEAN
S.D.	15.82	23.49	13.63	25.13	10.49	13.01	13.93	23.05	S.D.

Grade 11 thru ADULT Table 2.11- Volume 2 Conversion of Raw Scores to Scaled Scores

Scaled Score	VSTM	ASTM	VAPP	STM	STIMCMP RATIO	WRK-MEM LETTERS	WRKMEM WORDS	IMPULSE	Scaled Score
1	0-7	0-7	0-5	0-21	0-9	0-3	0-1	0-2	1
2	8-12	8-14	6-12	22-47	10-22	4-9	2-5	3-4	2
3	13-16	15-16	13-16	48-60	23-33	10-17	6	5	3
4	17-18	17-18	17-20	61-73	34-42	18-20	7-8	6	4
5	19-22	19-21	21-22	74-86	43-50	21-24	9-10	7	5
6	23-24	22-25	23	87-93	51-54	25-27	11-12	8-9	6
7	25-27	26-28	24-27	94-98	55-59	28-30	13-14	10-11	7
8	28-30	29-31	28-29	99-102	60-63	31-32	15-16	12	8
9	31-32	32-33	30-31	103-107	64-68	33-34	17-19	13-14	9
10	33-34	34-35	32-33	108-111	69-72	35-37	20	15-16	10
11	35-36	36	34-35	112-115	73-76	38	21	17-18	11
12	37-38	37-38	36-37	116-118	77-80	39-40	22-23	19-23	12
13	39-41	39-40	38	119-122	81-85	41	24-25	24-26	13
14	42	41	39	123-125	85-88	42	26-28	27-30	14
15	43-44	42-43	40	126-128	89-94	43	29-33	31-40	15
16	45	44	41	129	95-102	44	34-35	41-51	16
17	46	45	42-43	130-134	103-111	45	36-44	52-76	17
18	47-48	46-48	44-45	135-139	112-136	46-47	45+	76+	18
19			46+	140+	137+	48			19
'N'	1465	246	252	136	1098	167	730	220	'N'
r_{tt}	.81	.82	.81	.92	.86	.82	.77	.85	r_{tt}
C_{90}	.72	.75	.72	1.12	.84	.75	.66	.82	C_{90}
S.E.M.	3.07	2.55	2.31	4.06	5.29	2.71	3.19	3.38	S.E.M.
M.S.D.	6	5	5	8	11	6	7	7	M.S.D.
MEAN	33.24	36.47	34.44	108.52	70.18	35.53	18.69	15.35	MEAN
S.D.	6.84	4.91	5.30	14.00	14.36	6.36	6.66	8.56	S.D.

Grade 11-Adult Table 2.11- Volume 2   Conversion of Raw Scores to Scaled Scores

Scaled Scores	REHEARSE	CROSS MODAL	STIMULUS MODE*	RESPONSE MODE*	STM-MEM SEQUENCE	WRK-MEM SEQUENCE	STIMULUS NUMBER	SEQUENCE BY NUMBR	Scaled Scores
1	0-31	0-18	0-20	0-6	0-9	0-8	0-20	1-10	1
2	32-72	19-55	21-49	7-16	10-38	9-18	21-50	11-22	2
3	73-81	56-67	50-67	17-36	39-59	19-24	51-53	23-29	3
4	82-86	68-75	68-77	37-42	51-54	25-27	54-55	30-35	4
5	87-89	76-83	78-81	43-46	55-58	28-30	56-58	36-43	5
6	90-94	84-87	82-86	47-48	58-62	31-35	59-60	44-47	6
7	95-99	88-95	87-91	49-54	63-67	36-42	61-64	48-57	7
8	100-102	96-98	92-96	55-63	68-70	43-46	65-66	58-62	8
9	103-105	99-104	97-98	64-68	71-75	47-50	67-70	63-70	9
10	106-109	105-109	99-102	69-74	76-79	51-54	71-74	71-77	10
11	110-114	110-115	103-106	75-80	80-81	55-59	75-79	78-81	11
12	115-119	116-121	107-111	81-86	82-83	60-64	80-84	82-91	12
13	120-126	122-131	112-116	87-95	84-86	65-68	85-91	92-103	13
14	127-132	132-136	117-119	96-113	87-88	69-70	92-97	104-110	14
15	133-144	137-144	120-125	114-133	89-91	71-72	98-106	111-123	15
16	145-154	145-176	126-132	134-139	92-93	73-75	107-111	124-130	16
17	155-163	177-209	133-141	140-157	94-98	76-79	112-120	131-133	17
18	164-186	210-260	142-155	158-214	99-100	80-82	121-129	134-140	18
19	187+	261+	156+	215+		83+	130+	141+	19
N'	377	1791	389	149	218	218	377	159	N'
r_tt	.83	.85	.81	.94	.88	.92	.93	.96	r_tt
C_90	.79	.82	.72	1.32	.91	1.12	1.19	1.83	C_90
S.E.M.	6.56	8.99	5.87	6.34	3.64	3.67	3.82	4.68	S.E.M.
M.S.D.	13	18	12	13	8	8	8	9	M.S.D.
MEAN	110.35	110.07	101.53	75.40	74.69	52.78	75.36	75.60	MEAN
S.D.	15.82	23.49	13.63	25.13	10.49	13.01	13.93	23.05	S.D.

Appendix C

Individual

Visual-Written
Short Term

Examiner's Directions

INITIAL DIRECTIONS :

General Overview:

If Short-Term Memory Processes is the initial assessment Volume and more than one Volume is to be tested, use the following introduction.

SAY- We are going to do several tasks to see how you learn best. These tasks will help us plan your work to help you learn better.

SAY- Some of these tasks will be easy, others will be hard. Do the best you can on each task. You are not expected to answer every question, but try to do as well as you can.

SAY- Write your name, grade, age, birthday, and teachers name on the front page of your answer sheet.

WAIT: Until the learner has completed filling in the page. (observe how this is done.)

If the learner has serious difficulty, note this, and fill out, or help the learner fill out the identification page.

Volume 2. Task 1

VSTM Visual-Written Short Term Memory

SAY- We are going to do a group of tasks to see how well you remember.

SAY- This is a task to see how well you remember things that you see.

SAY- I am going to show you some letters, one at a time. When I finish, you write as many of them as you remember down the first column on your paper.

(demonstrate by pointing to the first column and running your finger down.

SAY-   Are there any questions?

If there are questions, repeat the instructions. and demonstrate, if necessary.

Then **:   SAY-   Put your pencils down**

SAY-Watch carefully or **Ready?**

Present-   The letters (words) one at a time in sequence for **two (2) seconds** each

Observe-The learner for signs of the method he or she is using to process the letters,

After the presentation of the third (3rd) letter:

Present letters in capital form, one at a time (2 seconds) on a separate stimulus flash card.

SAY-I am going to show you three (five, seven, nine), letters,(words) one at a time. When I finish, you write as many of them as you remember down the first column on your paper. (demonstrate by pointing to the first column and running your finger down.

M

VSTM- Visual Short Term Memory
Three Letters, Number 1
2 seconds

N

VSTM- Visual Short Term Memory
Three Letters, Number 2
2 seconds

W

VSTM- Visual Short Term Memory

Three Letters, Number 3

2 seconds

3. Letters **M - Z - W**

SAY-Write as many of those letters (words) as you can remember, in the first column of your answer sheet.

Wait-Till done, or 45 seconds

SAY-I am going to show you five, letters, one at a time. When I finish, you write as many of them as you remember down the second column on your paper. (demonstrate by pointing to the first column and running your finger down.

I

VSTM- Visual Short Term Memory
Five Letters, Number 1
2 seconds

VSTM- Visual Short Term Memory
Five Letters, Number 2
2 seconds

工

VSTM- Visual Short Term Memory
Five Letters, Number 3
2 seconds

F

VSTM- Visual Short Term Memory
Five Letters, Number 4
2 seconds

A

VSTM- Visual Short Term Memory

Five Letters, Number 5

2 seconds

5. Letters **I – K – H – F – A**

SAY-Write as many of those letters (words) as you can remember, in the second column of your answer sheet.

Wait-Till done, or 45 seconds

SAY-I am going to show you seven letters, one at a time. When I finish, you write as many of them as you remember down the Third column on your paper. (demonstrate by pointing to the first column and running your finger down.

B

VSTM- Visual Short Term Memory
Seven Letters, Number 1
2 seconds

N

VSTM- Visual Short Term Memory
Seven Letters, Number 2
2 seconds

P

VSTM- Visual Short Term Memory
Seven Letters, Number 3
2 seconds

T

VSTM- Visual Short Term Memory
Seven Letters, Number 4
2 seconds

C

VSTM- Visual Short Term Memory
Seven Letters, Number 5
2 seconds

E

VSTM- Visual Short Term Memory
Seven Letters, Number 6
2 seconds

VSTM- Visual Short Term Memory

Seven Letters, Number 7

2 seconds

7. Letters **B - N - P - T - C - E - Q**

SAY-Write as many of those letters (words) as you can remember, in the third column of your answer sheet.

Wait-Till done, or 45 seconds

SAY-I am going to show you nine letters,(words) one at a time. When I finish, you write as many of them as you remember down the fourth column on your paper. (demonstrate by pointing to the fourth column and running your finger down.

S

VSTM- Visual Short Term Memory
Nine Letters, Number 1
2 seconds

G

VSTM- Visual Short Term Memory
Nine Letters, Number 2
2 seconds

V

VSTM- Visual Short Term Memory
Nine Letters, Number 3
2 seconds

X

VSTM- Visual Short Term Memory
Nine Letters, Number 4
2 seconds

○

VSTM- Visual Short Term Memory
Nine Letters, Number 5
2 seconds

R

VSTM- Visual Short Term Memory

Nine Letters, Number 6

2 seconds

VSTM- Visual Short Term Memory
Nine Letters, Number 7
2 seconds

D

VSTM- Visual Short Term Memory
Nine Letters, Number 8
2 seconds

Y

VSTM- Visual Short Term Memory

Nine Letters, Number 9

2 seconds

9. Letters **S - G - V - X - O - R -J - D - Y**

SAY-Write as many of those letters (words) as you can remember, in the fourth column of your answer sheet.

Wait–Till done, or 45 seconds

Answer sheets p. ??

Volume 2. Task 1
VSTM - WORDS

SAY-This is a task to see how well you remember words that you see.

SAY-I am going to show you some words, one at a time. When I finish showing all of them, you write as many of them as you remember down the first column on your paper. (demonstrate by pointing to the first column and running your finger down.

SAY-Are there any questions?

If there are questions, repeat the instructions. and demonstrate, if necessary.

Then:**SAY- Put your pencils down**

SAY-Watch carefully or **Ready?**

Present–The letters (words) one at a time in sequence for **two (2) seconds** each

Observe–The learner for signs of the method he or she is using to process the letters,

I am going to show you three words, when I finish, you write all you can remember in the first column.

SIZE

VSTM- Visual Short Term Memory
Three Words, Number 1
2 seconds

LOCK

VSTM- Visual Short Term Memory
Three Words, Number 2
2 seconds

RULE

VSTM - Visual Short Term Memory

Three Words, Number 3

2 seconds

3. Words **SIZE - LOCK - RULE**

SAY-Write as many of those letters (words) as you can remember, in the third column of your answer sheet.

Wait-Till done, or 45 seconds

I am going to show you five words, when I finish, you write all you can remember in the second column.

FACT

VSTM- Visual Short Term Memory
Five Words, Number 1
2 seconds

DISH

VSTM- Visual Short Term Memory
Five Words, Number 2
2 seconds

COPY

VSTM- Visual Short Term Memory
Five Words, Number 3
2 seconds

SORT

VSTM- Visual Short Term Memory
Five Words, Number 4
2 seconds

ROOF

VSTM- Visual Short Term Memory

Five Words, Number 1

2 seconds

5. Words **FACT - DISH - COPY - SORT - ROOF**

SAY-Write as many of those letters (words) as you can remember, in the third column of your answer sheet.

Wait-Till done, or 45 seconds

I am going to show you seven words, when I finish, you write all you can remember in the first column.

BELT

VSTM- Visual Short Term Memory

Seven Words, Number 1

2 seconds

RAIL

VSTM- Visual Short Term Memory

Seven Words, Number 2

2 seconds

STEP

VSTM- Visual Short Term Memory

Seven Words, Number 3

2 seconds

FORK

VSTM- Visual Short Term Memory
Seven Words, Number 4
2 seconds

INCH

VSTM- Visual Short Term Memory
Seven Words, Number 5
2 seconds

WAND

VSTM- Visual Short Term Memory
Seven Words, Number 6
2 seconds

DOCK

VSTM- Visual Short Term Memory

Seven Words, Number 7

2 seconds

7. Words **BELT - RAIL - STEP - FORK - INCH - WAND - DOCK**

SAY-Write as many of those letters (words) as you can remember, in the third column of your answer sheet.

Wait-Till done, or 45 seconds

I am going to show you nine words, when I finish, you write all you can remember in the first column.

-233-

TAXI

VSTM- Visual Short Term Memory
Nine Words, Number 1
2 seconds

SOIL

VSTM- Visual Short Term Memory
Nine Words, Number 2
2 seconds

PULP

VSTM- Visual Short Term Memory
Nine Words, Number 3
2 seconds

AREA

VSTM- Visual Short Term Memory
Nine Words, Number 4
2 seconds

CENT

VSTM- Visual Short Term Memory
Nine Words, Number 5
2 seconds

GIFT

VSTM- Visual Short Term Memory
Nine Words, Number 6
2 seconds

TYPE

VSTM- Visual Short Term Memory
Nine Words, Number 7
2 seconds

BUST

VSTM- Visual Short Term Memory
Nine Words, Number 8
2 seconds

NOTE

VSTM- Visual Short Term Memory

Nine Words, Number

2 seconds

9. WordsTAXI - SOIL - PULP - AREA - CENT - GIFT - TYPE - BUST - NOTE

SAY-Write as many of those letters (words) as you can remember, in the fourth column of your answer sheet.

Wait–Till done, or 45 seconds

Appendix D

Individual

Auditory-
Written
Short Term
Memory

ASTM Auditory-

Written Short Term
Memory for letters

SAY- This is a task to see how well you remember things that you hear.

SAY- I am going to say letters, one at a time. When I finish, you write as many of them as you remember down the first column on your paper. (demonstrate by pointing to the first column and running your finger down.

SAY-Are there any questions? If there are questions, repeat the instructions. and demonstrate,

SAY-   Listen carefully

Present-   The letters one at a time in sequence for two (2) seconds each. Use a clear flat voice with no inflection. Be sure the presentation rate is even, do not group or chunk or inflect the letters.

This time there will be three letters, one at a time, when I finish all three, you write as many as you remember in the first column on your answer sheet

     SAY-   N - P - F in a clear voice, 2 seconds each

     SAY-   Write as many as you can remember in the first column of you answer sheet.

     Wait-   Till done, or 45 seconds

This time there will be five letters, one at a time, when I finish all five,

you write as many as you remember in the second column in your answer sheet

5 Letters **A - V - M - T - I**,(two seconds each letter)

SAY-Write as many as you can remember in the first column of you answer sheet.

Wait-   Till done, or 45 seconds

This time there will be seven letters, one at a time, when I finish all seven, you write as many as you remember in the third column in your answer sheet

7 Letters **B - G - D - L - H - J - Z**

SAY- Write as many as you can remember in the first column of you answer sheet.

Wait - Till done, or 45 seconds

This time there will be nine letters, one at a time, when I finish all nine, you write as many as you remember in the fourth column in your answer sheet

9 Letters **U - C - R - K - W - S - Y - O - E**

SAY- Write as many as you can remember in the first column of you answer sheet.

Wait- Till done, or 45 seconds

Answer sheets see p.101

ASTM- WORDS

repeat directions with the following words.

SAY-This is a task to see how well you remember words that you hear.

This time there will be three words, one at a time, when I finish all three you write as many as you remember in the first column in your answer sheet

3 Words **OVEN - RAKE - POND**

SAY-Write as many as you can remember in the first column of you answer sheet.

Wait- Till done, or 45 seconds

This time there will be five words, one at a time, when I finish all five, you write as many as you remember in the Second column in your answer sheet

5 Words **GIFT - VIEW - HEAT - RAFT - FADE**

SAY- Write as many as you can remember in the first column of you answer sheet.

Wait- Till done, or 45 seconds

This time there will be seven words, one at a time, when I finish all seven, you write as many as you remember in the third column in your answer sheet

7 Words **CROP - MAST - HEAL - SOCK - NEAR - FLED - REST**

SAY- Write as many as you can remember in the first column of you answer sheet.

Wait- seconds   Till done, or 45

This time there will be nine words, one at a time, when I finish all nine, you write as many as you remember in the fourth column in your answer sheet

9 Words **SOAK - FLIP - PEST - NOSE - STOP - RUTS - MOPE - NAIL - GAZE**

SAY-Write as many as you can remember in the first column of you answer sheet.

Wait- Till done, or 45 seconds

Appendix E

Visual-Written

Apprehension Span

VAPP   Visual Apprehension Span

SPECIFIC DIRECTIONS

Prepare four cards with the 3, 5, 7, or 9 letter stimuli in capital letter

SAY-This is a test to see how well you remember groups of letters that you see.

SAY-I am going to show you a card with 3 letters (words) on it. You write all of those letters (words) you remember, in the first column of your answer sheet, as soon as I put down the card.

SAY- Are there any questions?

If there are questions, repeat the instructions. and, demonstrate, if necessary.

SAY - Put your pencils down

SAY-Watch carefully or **Ready?**

Flash Each card of 3, 5, 7, or 9 letters (or Words) is presented for two (2) seconds and then placed face down where the letters or words cannot be seen by the learner.

RSY

VAPP- Visual Apprehension Span Card 1

Three Letters,

2 seconds

SAY-Write as many of those letters as you can remember, in the first column of your answer sheet.

Wait-Till done, or 45 seconds

I am going to show you five words,
when I finish, you write all you can remember in the second column.

P K Y E U

VAPP- Visual Apprehension Span Card 2

Five Letters,

2 seconds

SAY-Write as many of those letters as you can remember, in the first column of your answer sheet.

Wait-Till done, or 45 seconds

I am going to show you seven letters, when I finish, you write all the letters you can remember in the second column.

FNHDTAQ

VAPP- Visual Apprehension Span Card 3

Seven Letters,

2 seconds

**SAY-Write as many of those letters as you can remember,
in the first column of your answer sheet.**

Wait-Till done, or 45 seconds

**I am going to show you nine letters,
when I finish, you write all the letters
you can remember in the second column.**

O V C W B

I J L G

VAPP- Visual Apprehension Span Card 4

Nine Letters,

2 seconds

SAY-Write as many of those letters as you can remember, in the fourth column of your answer sheet.

Wait Till done, or 45 seconds

SAY-I am going to show you a card with 3 words on it. You write all of those letters (words) you remember, in the first column of your answer sheet, as soon as I put down the card.

SAY- Are there any questions?

If there are questions, repeat the instructions. and, demonstrate, if necessary.

SAY- Put your pencils down

SAY-Watch carefully or Ready?

Flash Each card of 3, 5, 7, or 9 Words, presented for two (2) seconds and then placed face down where the words cannot be seen by the learner.

SHOP LOGS RENT

VAPP- Visual Apprehension Span Card 5

Three Words,

2 seconds

SAY-Write as many of those letters as you can remember,
in the first column of your answer sheet.

Wait-Till done, or 45 seconds

I am going to show you five words,
when I finish, you write all the words
you can remember in the second column.

CROP NAVY PATH

LOAD BOOT

Visual Apprehension Span Card 6

Five words,

2 seconds

SAY-Write as many of those letters as you can remember, in the first column of your answer sheet.

Wait-Till done, or 45 seconds

I am going to show you seven words, when I finish, you write all the words you can remember in the third column.

RACK TRAP VASE
PORT BATH FUEL
GRIP

VAPP- Visual Apprehension Span Card 7

Seven Letters,

2 seconds

SAY-Write as many of those letters as you can remember, in the first column of your answer sheet.

Wait-Till done, or 45 seconds

I am going to show you nine letters, when I finish, you write all the letters you can remember in the fourth column.

COOP PINE SAIL

MANE RANK BASE

TRAP VALE PIPE

VAPP- Visual Apprehension Span Card 8

Nine Letters,

2 seconds

SAY-Write as many of those letters as you can remember,
in the first column of your answer sheet.

Wait-Till done, or 45 seconds

Appendix F
Individual

Auditory-Verbal

Short Term Memory

AVSTM Auditory-Verbal Short-Term Memory

SAY- This is a task to see how well you remember letters that you hear. This task is like one before, except this time you tell me the letters you remember.

SAY- I am going to say three words, one at a time. When I finish, you tell me all the letters you remember.

SAY-   Are there any questions?

If there are questions, repeat the instructions. and   demonstrate, if necessary.

Then: **SAY-   Put your pencils down**

SAY-   Listen carefully

Present-   The letters one at a time in sequence for two (2) seconds each. Use a clear flat voice with no inflection. Be sure the presentation rate is even, do not group or chunk the letters.

Record - **The correct responses in <u>sequence</u> by numeral and the errors with hatch marks.**

The directions for administration of the words section of the Developmental Neuropsychological Assessment, Auditory Short Term Memory (ASTM) task are identical to those of the letter section except that **Words** is substituted for **letters** in the directions.

Directions for administrator: Number each letter or word as the respondent says it. If an error is made, make a mark in the error column. You may keep track of sequencing by writing the number for each response. In the box below record the number Correct, the number of Errors of commission, and the number of items in correct Sequence

Errors of commission are those responses where the learner says a word or letter that is **NOT** one of the stimuli presented

Present- The letters one at a time in sequence for two (2) seconds each. Use a clear flat voice with no inflection. Be sure the presentation rate is even, do not group or chunk or inflect the letters.

This time there will be three letters, one at a time, when I finish all three, you tell me as many as you remember.

SAY- **C-Z-A** in a clear voice, 2 seconds each

SAY- **Tell me as many as you can remember.**

Wait- Till done, or 45 seconds

is time there will be five letters, one at a time, when I finish all five, you tell me as many as you remember.

5 Letters **H-M-V-T-L**,(two seconds each letter)

SAY-Tell me as many as you can remember.

Wait-   Till done, or 45
seconds

This time there will be seven letters, one at a time, when I finish all seven, you tell me as many as you remember.

7 Letters **X-I-W-K-N-P-V** (two seconds each letter)

SAY- Tell me as many as you can remember.

Wait - Till done, or 45 seconds

This time there will be nine letters, one at a time, when I finish all nine, you tell me as many as you remember.

9 Letters **D-L-A-V-G-O-J-Q-I** (two seconds each letter)

SAY- **Tell me as many as you can remember.**

Wait- Till done, or 45 seconds

Answer sheets see p.301

ASTM- WORDS

repeat directions with the following words.

SAY-This is a task to see how well you remember words that you hear.

This time there will be three words, one at a time, when I finish all three you tell me as many as you remember.

3 Words **SOCK-RINK-PALM** (two seconds each word.)

SAY-Tell me as many as you can remember.

Wait- Till done, or 45 seconds

This time there will be five words, one at a time, when I finish all five, you tell me as many as you remember.

5 Words **FORT-BUSH-ROOF-
CART- MASK** (two
seconds each word.)

SAY- Write as many as you can remember in the first column of you answer sheet.

Wait- Till done, or 45 seconds

This time there will be seven words, one at a time, when I finish all seven, you tell me as many as you remember.

7 Words **CURB-BONE-RACK-INCH-GIFT-LOAD- FORK** (two seconds each word.)

SAY- Tell me as many as you can remember.

Wait- Till done, or 45 seconds

This time there will be nine words, one at a time, when I finish all nine, you write as many as you remember in the fourth column in your answer sheet

9 Words **SOAK - FLIP - PEST - NOSE - STOP - RUTS - MOPE - NAIL - GAZE** (two seconds each word.)

SAY-Write as many as you can remember in the first column of you answer sheet.

Wait- Till done, or 45 seconds

II Examiner Record Forms
Volume 2- D Task 4. AVSTM
Auditory-Verbal Short-Term Memory
Presentation rate **2 seconds** per word
AVSTM Stimulus Letters

1. C ___	1. H ___	1. X ___	1. D ___
2. Z ___	2. M ___	2. I ___	2. L ___
3. A ___	3. V ___	3. W ___	3. A ___
	4. T ___	4. K ___	4. V ___
	5. L ___	5. N ___	5. G ___
		6. P ___	6. P ___
		7. V ___	7. J ___
			8. Q ___
			9. I ___

	C	E	S
TOTAL			

Examiners Record Form
AVSTM Stimulus Words

1. SOCK ___	1. FORT ___	1. CURB ___	1. VINE ___
2. RINK ___	2. BUSH ___	2. BONE ___	2. POND ___
3. PALM ___	3. ROOF ___	3. RACK ___	3. CRIB ___
	4. CART ___	4. INCH ___	4. TANK ___
	5. MASK ___	5. GIFT ___	5. CORK ___
		6. LOAD ___	6. LOCK ___
		7. FORK ___	7. FUEL ___
			8. RAKE ___
			9. SIGN ___

	C	E	S
Total			

Appendix G

Individual

Visual-Verbal Simultaneous

Apprehension Span

VVAPP   Visual-Verbal Apprehension Span

SPECIFIC DIRECTIONS
Prepare four cards with the 3, 5, 7, or 9 letter stimuli in capital letter form.

SAY- This is a test to see how well you remember groups things that you see. This task is like one before, except this time you tell me the letters (words) you remember.

SAY- I am going to show you a card with 3 letters (words) on it. When I put the card down, you tell me all the letters (words) you remember.

SAY-   Are there any questions?If there are questions, repeat the instructions. and demonstrate, if necessary.

Then: **SAY- Watch carefully or Ready?**
Each card of 3, 5, 7, or 9 letters (or Words) is presented for two (2) seconds and then placed face down where the letters or words cannot be seen by the learner.

The responses are recorded by the examiner on the Examiner's Record Form using numerals to indicate sequence and hatch marks to indicate errors.

2 TASK-5   **VISUAL-VERBAL SHORT-TERM MEMORY.**

Directions for examiner: Mark or cross out each letter or word as the respondent says it. If an error is made, make a mark in the error column. You may keep track of sequencing by writing the number for each response. Record the number Correct, the number of Errors of commission and the number of items in correct Sequence

I am going to show you THREE LETTERS, when I finish, you say to me all the letters you can remember.

W L Q

VVAPP- Visual Apprehension Span Card 1

Three letters,

2 seconds

SAY-Say as many of those letters as you can remember.

Wait-Till done, or 45 seconds

I am going to show you FIVE LETTERS, when I finish, you say back to me all the letters you can remember.

AJFTN

VAPP- Visual Apprehension Span Card 2

Five letters,

2 seconds

SAY- Say as many of those letters as you can remember,

Wait–Till done, or 45 seconds

I am going to show you seven letters, when I finish, you say back to me all the letters you can remember

D M H Y O S G

VAPP- Visual Apprehension Span Card 3

Seven Letters,

2 seconds

SAY-Say as many of those letters as you can remember,

Wait-Till done, or 45 seconds

I am going to show you nine letters, when I finish, you say back to me all the words you can remember.

E B G J C

V L U H

VAPP- Visual Apprehension Span Card 4

Nine Letters,

2 seconds

SAY-Say as many of those letters as you can remember,

Wait-Till done, or 45 seconds

VVAPP WORDS

SAY-I am going to show you a card with 3 words on it. When I put the card down, you tell me all the letters words you remember.

GIRL BALL PICK

VVAPP- Visual Apprehension Span Card 1

Three Words

2 seconds

SAY-Say as many of those letters as you can remember.

Wait-Till done, or 45 seconds

I am going to show you FIVE words. When I finish, you say back to me all the letters you can remember.

DOLL GIVE MISS

FARM STOP

VVAPP- Visual Apprehension Span Card 2Five Words

2 seconds

SAY-Say as many of those letters as you can remember.

Wait-Till done, or 45 seconds

I am going to show you seven words. When I finish, you say back to me all the letters you can remember.

BACK MILK LAND

WARM TALK HAND

STEP

VVAPP- Visual Apprehension Span Card 2 Seven Words

2 seconds

SAY-Say as many of those letters as you can remember.

Wait-Till done, or 45 seconds

I am going to show you nine words. When I finish, you say back to me all the letters you can remember

WORK BIRD SWIM

FLAG HALL STAR

CLUB DESK ROCK

Volume II-E   Task 5
VVAPPVisual-Verbal Apprehension Span
Presentation rate 2 seconds per STIMULUS CARD

VVAPPStimulus Letters

1. W ____	1. A ____	1. D ____	1.E ____
2. L____	2. J ____	2. M ____	2. B ____
3. Q____	3. F____	3. H ____	3. G ____
	4. T____	4. Y ____	4. J ____
	5. N ____	5. O ____	5. C ____
		6. S ____	6. V ____
		7. G ____	7. L ____
			8.U ____
			9. H ____

	C	E	S
Total			

Visual-Verbal Apprehension Span

VVAPP Stimulus Words

1. GIRL ___   1. DOLL___   1. BACK ___   1. WORK___

2. BALL ___   2. GIVE ___
                             2. MILK ___   2. BIRD ___
3. PICK ___   3. MISS ___
                             3. LAND ___   3. SWIM ___
               4. FARM __

                             4. WARM __   4. FLAG ___
               5. STOP ___

                             5. TALK ___   5. HALL ___

                             6. HAND___   6. STAR ___

                             7. STEP ___
                                            7. CLUB___

                                            8. DESK___

                                            9. ROCK __

	C	E	S
Total			

Appendix H

Short Term Memory Student Answer Forms

Examiner Forms and Scoring

STUDENT ANSWER FORM
Volume 2 SHORT TERM MEMORY
Task 2 **Visual** Sequential Memory (VSTM Letters)

1. _____   1. _____   1. _____   1. _____

2. _____   2. _____   2. _____   2. _____

                 3. _____   3. _____   3. _____
3. _____
                 4. _____   4. _____   4. _____

                 5. _____   5. _____   5. _____

                                  6. _____   6. _____

                                  7. _____   7. _____

                                                   8. _____

                                                   9. _____

	C	E	S
Total			

STUDENT ANSWER FORM

Volume 6 Task I **Visual** Sequential Memory (VSTM, Words)

1. _____	1. _____	1. _____	1. _____
2. _____	2. _____	2. _____	2. _____
3. _____	3. _____	3. _____	3. _____
	4. _____	4. _____	4. _____
	5. _____	5. _____	5. _____
		6. _____	6. _____
		7. _____	7. _____
			8. _____
			9. _____

	C	E	S
Total			

STUDENT ANSWER FORM

Volume 6 Task 2 **Auditory** Sequential Memory (ASTM Letters)

1. _____	1. _____	1. _____	1._____
2. _____	2. _____	2. _____	2. _____
3. _____	3. _____	3. _____	3. _____
	4. _____	4. _____	4. _____
	5. _____	5. _____	5. _____
		6. _____	6. _____
		7. _____	7. _____
			8. _____
			9. _____

	C	E	S
Total			

STUDENT ANSWER FORM

Volume 6 Task II **Auditory** Sequential Memory (ASTM Words)

1. _____   1. _____   1. _____   1._____

2. _____   2. _____   2. _____   2. _____

3. _____   3. _____   3. _____   3. _____

             4. _____   4. _____   4. _____

             5. _____   5. _____   5. _____

                        6. _____   6. _____

                        7. _____   7. _____

                                     8. _____

                                9. _____

	C	E	S
Total			

STUDENT ANSWER FORM
(Letters) **VAPP** Letters 3.
Volume 6 Task III Visual Simultaneous Memory VAPP Letters)

1. _____   1. _____   1. _____   1._____

2. _____   2. _____   2. _____   2. _____

3. _____   3. _____   3. _____   3. _____

              4. _____   4. _____   4. _____

              5. _____   5. _____   5. _____

                            6. _____   6. _____

                            7. _____   7. _____

                                          8. _____

                                          9. _____

	C	E	S
Total			

STUDENT ANSWER FORM
Volume 2 Task IV (Words) **VAPP** Words 3.
Visual Simultaneous Memory VAPP)

1. _____   1. _____   1. _____   1. _____

2. _____   2. _____   2. _____   2. _____

3. _____   3. _____   3. _____   3. _____

               4. _____   4. _____   4. _____

               5. _____   5. _____   5. _____

                               6. _____   6. _____

                               7. _____   7. _____

                                              8. _____

                                     9. _____

	C	E	S
Total			

-334-

II Examiner Record Forms
Volume 2- D Task 4. AVSTM
Auditory-Verbal Short-Term Memory
Presentation rate **2 seconds** per word
AVSTM Stimulus Letters

1. C ___	1. H ___	1. X ___	1. D ___
2. Z ___	2. M ___	2. I ___	2. L ___
3. A ___	3. V ___	3. W ___	3. A ___
	4. T ___	4. K ___	4. V ___
	5. L ___	5. N ___	5. G ___
		6. P ___	6. P ___
		7. V ___	7. J ___
			8. Q ___
			9. I ___

	C	E	S
TOTAL			

Examiners Record Form
AVSTM Stimulus Words

1. SOCK ___	1. FORT ___	1. CURB ___	1. VINE ___
2. RINK ___	2. BUSH ___	2. BONE ___	2. POND ___
3. PALM ___	3. ROOF ___	3. RACK ___	3. CRIB ___
	4. CART ___	4. INCH ___	4. TANK ___
	5. MASK ___	5. GIFT ___	5. CORK ___
		6. LOAD ___	6. LOCK ___
		7. FORK ___	7. FUEL ___
			8. RAKE ___
			9. SIGN ___

	C	E	S
Total			

Examiners Record Form
Volume 2-E Task 5
VVAPP Visual-Verbal
Apprehension Span
Presentation rate 2 seconds per STIMULUS CARD

VVAPP Stimulus Letters

1. W ___	1. A ___	1. D ___	1.E ___
2. L ___	2. J ___	2. M ___	2. B ___
3. Q ___	3. F ___	3. H ___	3. G ___
	4. T ___	4. Y ___	4. J ___
	5. N ___	5. O ___	5. C ___
		6. S ___	6. V ___
		7. G ___	7. L ___
			8.U ___
			9. H ___

	C	E	S
Total			

Examiners Record Form
Visual-Verbal Apprehension Span

VVAPP Stimulus Words

1. GIRL ____ 1. DOLL____ 1. BACK ____ 1. WORK____

2. BALL ____ 2. GIVE ____ 2. MILK ____ 2. BIRD ____

3. PICK ____ 3. MISS ____ 3. LAND ____ 3. SWIM ____

4. FARM ____ 4. WARM ____ 4. FLAG ____

5. STOP ____ 5. TALK ____ 5. HALL ____

6. HAND____ 6. STAR ____

7. STEP ____ 7. CLUB____

8. DESK____

9. ROCK ____

	C	E	S
Total			

Examiners Work Sheet

Volume II **Processing in Short-Term Memory**

   Measure   Formation   Raw   Total Scaled

                                Score Score Score

2.1 VISUAL SHORT-TERM MEMORY (VSTM)

(VSTM letters   _____

plus VSTM words)   __   __   __

2.2 AUDITORY SHORT-TERM MEMORY (ASTM)

        (ASTM letters   __

    plus ASTM words)   __   __   __

2.3 VISUAL APPREHENSION SPAN (VAPP)

(VAPP letters   __

      plus VAPP words) __   __   __

2.4 SHORT-TERM MEMORY TOTAL (STM)

        (VSTM TOTAL   __

plus ASTM TOTAL   __

plus VAPP TOTAL   __   __   __

2.5* AUDITORY-VERBAL SHORT TERM MEMORY (AVSTM)*

     AVSTM letters   ____

     plus ASTM words ____ ____   ____

Volume II   Processing in Short-Term Memory

Measure	Formation	Raw Score	Total Score	Scaled Score

2.6* VISUAL-VERBAL SHORT TERM MEMORY (VVSTM*

VVSTM letters   ____

plus VVSTM words   ____   ____   ____

2.7 STIMULUS COMPLEXITY RATIO (STIMCOMP)

((VSTM words __

plus VAPP words)+1)   __

divided by((VSTM letters   ____

plus VAPP letters)+1)*100   __   __   ____

use scaled scores for VSTM as a basis for comparison.

2.8. WORKING MEMORY, LETTERS (WKMEML)

(VSTM, 7+9 letters   ____

plus   ASTM, 7+9 letters   __

plus   VAPP, 7+9 letters   ____   ____   ____

2.9 FUNCTIONAL MEMORY CAPACITY FOR LETTERS

Total Working
Memory for Letters   ____

Divided by   6   ____   ____   ____

2.10. WORKING MEMORY, WORDS (WKMEMW)

(VSTM, 7+9 words   ____

plus   ASTM, 7+9 words   ____

plus   VAPP, 7+9 words   ____ ____ ____

2.11 FUNCTIONAL MEMORY CAPACITY FOR WORDS

Total Working
Memory for Words   ____

Divided by   6   ____ ____ ____

2.12. IMPULSIVITY (IMPULSE)

((VSTM Errors   ____

Plus   ASTM Errors   ____

Plus   VAPP Errors+1)   ____ ____

Divided by (STM+1))*100   ____ ____ ____

2.13 REHEARSAL EFFECTS (REHEARSE)

((VSTM Total+1)   ____

Divided by(VAPP Total+1))*100 ____ ____ ____

Volume II   Processing in Short-Term Memory

Measure   Formation   Raw   Total   Scaled

Score   Score   Score

2.14 CROSS MODAL EFFICIENCY (CROSMODE)

((ASTM Total   _____

Plus   VVAPP Total+1)   _____ _____

Divided by (AVSTM Total   _____

Plus   VSTM Total+1))*100 _____ _____ _____

2.15 STIMULUS MODE (STIMMODE)

((ASTM Total   _____

plus   AVSTM Total+1)   _____ _____

divided by (VSTM Total   _____

plus VVAPP Total+1))*100 _____ _____ _____

Higher scores indicate verbal stimulus advantage

2.16 RESPONSE MODE (RESPMODE)

((AVSTM Total   _____

plus   VVAPP Total+1)   _____ _____

divided by   ASTM Total   _____

plus VAPP TOTAL+1))*100 _____ _____ _____

2.17 MEMORY RESPONSE SEQUENCING (MEMSEQ)

((VSTM, SEQ Total _____

plus   ASTM, SEQ Total   _____

plus   VAPP, SEQ Total+1)_____ _____

divided by

(STM Total+1))*100 ____ ____ ____

Volume II   Processing in Short-Term Memory
  Measure   Formation   Raw Total
Scaled

                               Score Score

Score

2.18 WORKING MEMORY SEQUENCING
(WKMEMSEQ)

((VSTM,SEQ 7+9 WORD   ____
plus ASTM,SEQ 7+9 WORDS   ____
plus VAPP,SEQ 7+9 WORDS+1) ____ ____
divided by
(WORKMEM WORDS+1))*100   ____ ____ ____

2.19 STIMULUS NUMBER EFFECTS
(STIMNUMB)

          ((VSTM 3+5 LTRS ____
plus   VSTM 3+5 WRDS ____
plus   ASTM 3+5 LTRS ____
plus   ASTM 3+5 WRDS ____
plus   VAPP 3+5 LTRS ____
plus   VAPP 3+5 WRDS+1) ____ ____
divided by
(ΣWORK MEM LETTERS____
WORKMEM WORDS+1))*100 ____ ____ ____

2.20 STIMULUS NUMBER SEQUENCING EFFECT
(SEQNUMBR)
$\sum$ SEQ 7&9, Letters & Words+1)____

divided by

$\sum$ aSEQ 3&5, letters & words+1)*100 _____ _____ -

___